THE JUDGES

To Tom and Sue
With thanks for your
interest and support.

Paul Oale

THE JUDGES

PAUL OSLER

Matador
9 Priory Business Park,
Wistow Road, Kibworth Beauchamp,
Leicestershire. LE8 0RX
Tel: 0116 279 2299
Email: books@troubador.co.uk
Web: www.troubador.co.uk/matador
Twitter: @matadorbooks

ISBN 978 1789010 107

British Library Cataloguing in Publication Data.
A catalogue record for this book is available from the British Library.

Printed and bound by CPI Group (UK) Ltd, Croydon, CR0 4YY
Typeset in 11pt Minion Pro by Troubador Publishing Ltd, Leicester, UK

Matador is an imprint of Troubador Publishing Ltd

To my father – a man of honour.

"... makes your blood boil at the injustice."

Ian Winters, Ellis Winters Estate Agents, England.

"... a side of the legal profession I would never have believed existed... I kept thinking at every stage, each judge was so obviously covering the tracks of the other, that at some point the house of cards would fall down. The fact that all the players were venturing so far off base and still got away with it is astonishing."

Bryan Dunbar, Retired Retail Consultant, Scotland.

"It's a pity that the end couldn't have been that all the judges were sacked."

Tom Breese, Retired Civil Engineer, Wales.

CONTENTS

APPENDIX F: CORRESPONDENCE WITH THE MPs –

"To no one will we sell, to no one
deny or delay right or justice."

Clause 40, *Magna Carta*, 1215

"For in the same way you judge others,
you will be judged, and with the
measure you use, it will be measured to you."

Jesus of Nazareth

Matthew 7:2 (New International Version)

This is a true story.

PREFACE

"Help, master, help! here's a fish hangs
in the net, like a poor man's right in the law"

William Shakespeare, *Pericles* (2.1.117-118)

What do you think of the judges of England and Wales? Do you respect them? Do you fear them? Are they honest, respectful and wise? Are they hypocrites? Are they accountable?

What is a court? Is it a building like a Gothic cathedral, or an oak-panelled room where the players wear costumes, appear important and intelligent and are supported by officials in a prevailing atmosphere of authority and control? In truth, surely a court can be any place where there is an honest attempt to apply the law and do justice. It could sit in a barn with judges who have straw in their hair and cow-dirt on their wellies. The essence of a court is what is said and done; the rest is trimming, our homage to justice. In a court, you should feel able to say what you want to say, be it right or wrong, without being ridiculed or bullied.

When I qualified as a solicitor in 1992, I never dreamt that twenty-three years later I would make allegations of dishonesty against three of Her Majesty's judges, yet that is what has happened. Having founded Oslers Solicitors[1] in 1997, a firm which still exists with offices in Suffolk and Cambridgeshire; having in 2006 and 2007 represented Steven Wright, the so-called Suffolk Strangler; and having been retired for seven years, yet still in my mid-fifties; in a court case conducted for a friend, I would find my arguments, if not myself, treated with contempt by a sequence of three judges against whom I felt compelled to make extraordinary accusations.

In this book, I am going to take you through that court case and my allegations, but my main purpose is not to persuade you that the latter are true, even though they represent my honest opinion. Rather, it is to raise relevant and important questions in the public interest about the power, integrity and accountability of our judges and to ask you to form your own opinion.

Financial disputes of £10,000 or less are normally dealt with in court as "small claims" and they receive a more informal and swifter treatment. Most of the disputes which the majority of us will face will be small claims. Rarely, if ever, will there be a journalist or legal commentator present at the trial. Appeals are not usual. Often the parties are not legally represented. Effectively, these cases are off the publicity radar, and a judge might expect not to have her decision or conduct scrutinised. Yet perhaps it is in such cases we can learn most about the power and integrity of the judges, just as the measure of a person is found in what he or she does in the belief no one is watching. This book is about such a case.

I have used the word "dishonest" in relation to the decisions and actions of judges and civil servants. This does not refer to financial dishonesty but, rather, to the deliberate making of false statements and incorrect decisions.

---

1   Oslers Solicitors has not been involved in the case which is the subject of this book, and the views expressed are mine alone.

If a judge dishonestly breaches her duty and, as a direct result, a person is denied money which he is lawfully entitled to, is the essence of that conduct different to that of the thief who snatches a purse from a woman? Perhaps the difference is that the thief does not pretend to be anything else; the judge, however, acts with state-licensed authority and power and wears a mask of decency.

It is important to say at the outset that not all judges are bad. There are many excellent judges, but this book is not about them; it is about the others and how the system fails to deal with them.

In this case, all of the judges were women, and, therefore, I have used the female gender when referring generally to a judge. On the other hand, the two house-purchasers were men, so I have used the male gender to refer generally to purchasers. In other cases, I have used the male gender.

I have used fictitious names and places, where appropriate, to maintain the privacy of my friend, but, subject to obvious safeguards and my friend's consent, I am willing to disclose the true details of the court, the case number and the parties should the request come from a senior judge[2], the police, a legal commentator, an academic or a media organisation. Should any fictitious name suggest the identity of an actual person or company, such is entirely unintentional and accidental. I have disclosed the real names of the Judicial Conduct Investigations Office employees, the Judicial Appointments and Conduct Ombudsman and the MPs.

Public documents are reproduced courtesy of the Open Government Licence (see http://www.nationalarchives.gov.uk/doc/open-government-licence/version/3/).

This is not intended to be a law textbook, and I have tried to avoid giving law references. I have provided them (at the end of each relevant section) only where I have considered it necessary.

---

2   Prior to the publication of this book, a copy was sent to the courts where the judges I criticise work, namely, the County Court and the High Court. I also disclosed to them the details of the real case which is the subject of the book. No response has been received.

INTRODUCTION

"The plaintiff and defendant in an action at law are two men ducking their heads in a bucket, and daring each other to remain longest under water."

Samuel Johnson (attributed to)

In 2013, my friend, John Smith, asked my advice on a solicitor's letter he had received demanding compensation on behalf of Roger Jones Ltd., a company of chartered surveyors owned by Roger Jones. John is an experienced chartered surveyor, and he had done work as an agent for Roger Jones Ltd., surveying houses and preparing reports for the purchasers. The letter stated that, in relation to two houses, John had not mentioned in his reports certain defects and the company had compensated the purchasers and incurred expenses. The company wanted reimbursement from John. And so it began.

THE DEMAND

"Crack the lawyer's voice,
That he may never more false title plead,
Nor sound his quillets shrilly."

William Shakespeare,
Timon of Athens (4.3.152-154)

The letter demanding John reimburse Roger Jones Ltd. came from Borders Solicitors.

Regarding 1 Elm Close, the letter stated that a survey report John had written for a Mr Freeman had not mentioned a woodworm infestation in the garage roof timbers. The woodworm treatment had cost £150, which the company had paid.

Regarding 5 Maple Avenue, the letter stated that a survey report John had written for a Mr Turner had mentioned neither some rotten wood in the conservatory nor a dripping shower. In the end, Mr Turner had been paid £1,250 by the company, which, in addition, had incurred an ombudsman's fee of £260.

Roger Jones Ltd. wanted John to pay it the £150, the £1,250, and the £260, a total of £1,660. If he did not pay, administrative costs of £100 would also be claimed in any court proceedings.

So, what was John to do?

It would have been easy for him to have accepted that the clients' complaints related to his reports and that, therefore, he should take responsibility for any compensation. But just because the complaints related to his reports did not mean he had been at fault or caused the clients to have incurred the costs complained of.

Although it was not a trivial sum, John could have paid the £1,660 just to avoid the aggravation of any dispute. Alternatively, he could have offered to pay some of it.

For reasons that will become clear later, John and I thought he had done nothing wrong. Even if he had, I advised him his reports had not left the company with any liability to the clients and he was not liable to reimburse the company.

There are also tactical reasons for rejecting a demand such as this. In court proceedings, a claim for this amount is almost certainly going to be treated as a small claim and special rules apply. One of those rules is that even a party who wins the case will not recover lawyers' fees from the losing party. There is an exception to this rule where the losing party has behaved unreasonably, but this is not commonly applied. It follows, where a party is using lawyers, its fees can very quickly amount to far more than it is seeking to recover in the dispute, so it is not worth pursuing. After all, who is going to spend £5,000 on lawyers' fees to recover £2,000 of damages? It seemed to me very unlikely Roger Jones Ltd. would instruct Borders Solicitors to conduct court proceedings to recover £1,760 since the unrecoverable legal fees would far exceed that sum. Also, the company would be admitting in a court that it had been negligent in relation to two clients! Although a retired solicitor, I could still assist John with his defence, and the law even allowed me to represent him

3

at a small claim trial. If John lost his case, he would have to pay the £1,760 and any court fees and expenses which Roger Jones Ltd. incurred, which I thought would be in the region of £500. The downside of fighting the demand seemed low. The demand was rejected. Roger Jones Ltd. sued, and Borders Solicitors was acting.

THE CLAIM

"Lawyers are the only persons in whom
ignorance of the law is not punished."

Jeremy Bentham (attributed to)

The claim form sent to the court starts the formal proceedings. That of Roger Jones Ltd. maintained John Smith had prepared survey reports for Mr Freeman and Mr Turner; in his reports he had not mentioned defects in the properties which he should have mentioned; therefore, he had been negligent; and the two purchasers had been compensated by the company in the amount of the cost of the repairs.

In relation to 1 Elm Close, it was said John Smith had not reported a woodworm infestation in the garage roof timbers.

In relation to 5 Maple Avenue, it was said John Smith had reported neither rotting wood in the conservatory roof timbers nor a constantly dripping shower unit.

The claim stated the company had been "obliged" to compensate the two purchasers.

The compensation paid by the company to Mr Freeman of 1 Elm Close had simply been the cost of treating the woodworm, namely £150. It was said that, having received a complaint from Mr Freeman, Roger Jones had visited the property and had "had no choice but to concede the existence of the infestation problem and fund the cost of professional treatment".

The compensation paid to Mr Turner had been more than just the cost of the repairs (the value of which was never clearly established since, as will be seen, Mr Turner had claimed widely different amounts in relation to both the conservatory and the shower and had not provided paid invoices). Having made his complaint to the company, Mr Turner, dissatisfied with the response received, had complained to the relevant ombudsman, which had resulted in the company paying a fee of £260. Roger Jones Ltd.'s claim stated the ombudsman had directed the company to pay Mr Turner £925 (which included reimbursement to him of his survey fee of £425) but Mr Turner had not accepted that resolution and had gone on to sue the company. Roger Jones Ltd.'s claim said that, acting on the recommendation of solicitors provided by the company's insurers, the company had settled Mr Turner's suit by paying him £1,250, which included Mr Turner's court fee of £70 and the return of the survey fee of £425 (so he had received £755 for the alleged defects to the conservatory and shower). It further stated, "At all times (Mr Turner) advanced his claims with vigour, and such settlement represented the best possible outcome that could reasonably have been achieved from (Roger Jones Ltd.'s) point of view."

In addition, Roger Jones Ltd. was asking for: "not less than £100" for administrative costs and out-of-pocket expenses; and interest on the sum of £1,760 at the daily rate of £0.39 (an annual rate of 8%), which at the time of issue amounted to £113.10.

When starting the proceedings, the company had paid a court fee of £115 and, since Borders Solicitors had prepared the claim form, £80 was claimed for legal representative costs.

In summary, the following was claimed by Roger Jones Ltd.:

1 Elm Close

Compensation to Mr Freeman	150.00
5 Maple Avenue	
Ombudsman fee	260.00
Compensation to Mr Turner	1,250.00
Admin costs /expenses	100.00
Interest	113.10
Court fee	115.00
Legal representative's costs	<u>80.00</u>
	<u>2,068.10</u>

So that was it. I hope at this stage it all seems pretty straightforward to you, and I wonder what your immediate thoughts are. Does it seem a clear-cut case against John Smith, or do you doubt part, or all, of the claim? Let's have a closer look.

THE DEFENCE

"Reason is the life of the law, nay the common
law is nothing else but reason."
Sir Edward Coke, *Institutes: Commentary upon Littleton*

Following receipt of a claim form, to contest the claim it is
necessary to file a written defence setting out the main arguments
as to why the claim is disputed.

In preparing a defence, it is necessary to consider all
possibilities. So even though you think your first argument is
enough to win the case, you must anticipate that, rightly or
wrongly, it will fail before the court, and you must prepare a
sequence of arguments until they are all included. Your defence
then becomes something like this: A (your first argument), but,
if that is incorrect, then B (your second argument), and, if not B,
then C... It is a belt and braces approach.

Had John Smith been negligent?

The claim maintained John Smith should have mentioned the relevant defects in his report, but was that right? What had been his duty exactly? Had it been, for example, to mention every defect present in the houses, or had it been something else and, if so, what? Negligence only occurs when a duty of care is breached, and it depends on what that duty is.

Common sense says a survey report is not going to mention every defect (e.g. minor plaster cracks) in a house since that would be an impossible task for a surveyor. Further, at the time of the surveys of 1 Elm Close and 5 Maple Avenue, there were two types of survey reports a purchaser could order from Roger Jones Ltd. These were a HomeBuyer Report and a Building Survey. The first valued the property and advised of defects which might affect the valuation, but it did not give cost estimates for repairs. The second was a more expensive and comprehensive report on the condition of the property, with a diagnosis of defects and repair needs. Both Mr Freeman and Mr Turner had chosen a HomeBuyer Report.

The HomeBuyer Report contract had been the same for both purchasers. It explained the report would identify what the surveyor considered to be the most important issues and would apply condition ratings to indicate whether defects were serious or urgent. It stated it "focuses on matters that, in the surveyor's opinion may affect the value of the property if they are not dealt with" and "any minor matters that do not affect the value of the property are generally not included". You can see the contractual duty was to give a reasonable valuation of the property and to mention significant defects. Further, it is obvious an expert's duty is to report on matters requiring his expertise – we do not need experts to tell us things we can know very well without their help.

So, should John Smith have mentioned the woodworm in the garage to Mr Freeman and the rotten timber in the conservatory and the dripping shower to Mr Turner? What did John Smith have to say about these defects?

John Smith had surveyed 1 Elm Close on behalf of Mr Freeman in December, but the woodworm was not reported until the following July and only then did Roger Jones inspect it. John Smith told me the woodworm had simply not been evident when he did his inspection in December.

Regarding the conservatory at 5 Maple Avenue, John Smith was not denying the defects had existed, but he had said in his survey report, "The timber-framed conservatory requires a number of repairs including the replacement of defective double-glazed seals and defective flashings and roof liners" and he had given it a condition rating of 3, the most serious, which the contract defined as, "Defects that are serious and/or need to be repaired or investigated urgently". He also told me that on the day of his inspection of the property, he had met Mr Turner there and had told him the conservatory was in poor repair and it would be expensive to fix it. Further, under the heading "What to do now", the survey report stated, "Before you make a legal commitment to buy the property, you should get reports and quotations for all the repairs and further investigations the surveyor may have identified" and "Condition rating 3 – repairs should be done as soon as possible."

Regarding the shower at 5 Maple Avenue, John Smith simply said it had not been dripping on the day of his survey inspection. On that day, he alone had entered the property. Roger Jones had not inspected the property at any time.

So, if the woodworm had not been visible at 1 Elm Close and the shower had not been dripping at 5 Maple Avenue at the time of the survey inspections, clearly, John Smith had not been at fault in not mentioning them in his report. Further, if the shower had been dripping at that time, why had Mr Turner not seen it prior to purchase since he surely had not needed an expert surveyor to tell him about that?

As for the conservatory timber, with a repair cost of about £600 in a house valued by John Smith at £348,000, should this defect have been mentioned specifically, or had John Smith highlighted sufficiently the general condition of the conservatory? He thought he had. Further, after Mr Turner had complained, Roger Jones had written to Mr Turner stating he was "satisfied the survey had been carried out for you in a proper manner" and he would "rigorously defend any allegations that we have not acted in accordance with the RICS (Royal Institution of Chartered Surveyors) Standard Terms of Engagement".

The question was not whether the report had been perfect or could have been better – the question was whether the report had been sufficient.

The defence was going to deny negligence.

If John Smith had been negligent, had that caused the house purchases?

Even if John Smith had been negligent, it was necessary to consider what losses, if any, Mr Freeman and Mr Turner had suffered for which the company had been "obliged" to compensate them, and then it was necessary to consider what losses the company had incurred over and above those suffered by the two purchasers and which might be claimed from John Smith.

It was not enough to say John Smith should have included the defects in his survey reports because, even if that was right, Mr Freeman and Mr Turner had only been entitled to compensation if, as a result, they had incurred a loss. If it had been a "no harm done" situation, the mistake would not have mattered.

It is important to bear in mind that a surveyor does not cause defects in a house. The defects are there, and the surveyor simply draws them to our attention. Most houses have defects which you can expect to inherit when buying, and there is a big difference between saying on the one hand, "I did not know about that defect" and on the other hand, "If I had known about it, I would not have bought the house". Further, there is a difference between saying, "I would not have bought the house" and "I bought it and I have suffered a loss". To be entitled to compensation, a purchaser must not only show the surveyor was negligent but also that, **as a consequence of that negligence**, a loss has been incurred.

It is a basic principle of law that if B is going to occur whether or not A occurs, A cannot be a cause of B. It is known as the "but for" principle. In other words, only if it can be said B would not have occurred "but for" A, can A be said to have been a cause of B (you can see "but for" means "if it hadn't been for"). It is not rocket science. Suppose my wife says to me, "If it doesn't rain today, I will water the garden". If it does not rain and she waters the garden, the fact it did not rain was a cause of her watering the garden. Now suppose she says, "Whether it rains or not today, I am going to water the garden". If it does not rain, that would not be a cause of her watering the garden because she was going to do it anyway – it cannot be said that "but for" the fact it did not rain, she would not have watered the garden.

In Mr Freeman's and Mr Turner's cases, it was necessary to ask whether they would still have bought the houses at the prices they had paid if they had known about the defects which they had complained were not in the survey reports. Bear in mind, at the time of receiving a survey report a purchaser will have incurred a survey fee, solicitors' fees and other property search fees, so if as a result of a survey report he pulls out of the purchase, he will have paid those fees with no house to show for them. For Mr Freeman and Mr Turner, those fees would have been at least £1,000 each. Would Mr Freeman have abandoned his purchase of 1 Elm Close, valued and bought at £320,000 (against an asking price of £325,000), if he had known of £150 of woodworm treatment? Would Mr Turner have abandoned his purchase of 5 Maple Avenue, valued at £348,000 and bought at £340,000 (against an asking price of £325,000), if he had known of £755 of repairs to the conservatory and the shower (the figure accepted by him upon the settlement of his claim against Roger Jones)? Remember, he had known from the survey report that the conservatory, which had been given a condition 3 rating, had defects which were serious and/or needed to be repaired or investigated urgently. No sensible person would write off £1,000 of fees because of £150 or £755 of repairs. So, it could not be said that "but for" John Smith not mentioning the defects, Mr Freeman and Mr Turner would not have bought their houses. These purchasers would have bought the houses at the same price even if the defects had been mentioned in the survey reports.

Further, in Mr Turner's case, he appeared to have been very keen to buy the property since he had paid £15,000 over the asking price. This was further evidence he would not have been put off his purchase by £755 of repairs.

Also in Mr Turner's case, the house had been valued by John Smith at £348,000 and Mr Turner had bought it for £340,000. He had been getting a bargain to the tune of £8,000 – all the more reason not to pull out of the purchase because of £755.

The defence would deny that any negligence by John Smith had led to Mr Freeman and Mr Turner buying their houses when they would not otherwise have done so.

Even if negligence by John Smith had been a cause of the house purchases, had any loss been incurred by the purchasers?

For argument's sake, suppose John Smith had been at fault and this meant Mr Freeman and Mr Turner had bought houses they would not otherwise have bought. It was still necessary to ask whether in buying the houses they had suffered a financial loss, a fact which could not be assumed.

Mr Freeman had bought a house valued by John Smith at £320,000 (a valuation not disputed by Roger Jones Ltd.), and that is what he paid for it. He discovered he had a £150 bill for woodworm treatment which he had not known about. So what? Was his house worth any less? Was it worth only £319,850? The question was this: was it legitimate to claim Mr Freeman's loss was the bill for £150, or was it necessary to show his house was worth less than he paid for it because of the £150? The first is known as the "cost of repairs" and the second as "diminution in value".

Why should his loss have been the £150 cost of repairs? Unlike a builder, a surveyor does not promise a house will be free of defects. The decisions of the higher courts have come down in favour of diminution in value being the loss to be considered in cases of negligence by a surveyor.

So, in order to establish financial loss, Mr Freeman would have needed to show that, as a result of a £150 repair, his house had been worth less than £320,000. House valuations are not so precise, and the courts have recognised that[1]. Mr Freeman's house had clearly not been worth less than he had paid for it just because of a £150 repair.

Mr Turner had bought a house valued by John Smith at £348,000 (a valuation not disputed by Roger Jones Ltd.), yet he had paid only £340,000 for it. So, he had got an £8,000 bargain. Had his house been worth less than £348,000 because of repairs of £755? Again, valuations are not so precise, and the answer was "no". Actually, it is very arguable that, for Mr Turner to have suffered a loss, the property would have had to have fallen below the value of £340,000.

For Roger Jones Ltd., there was a better argument relating to any financial loss Mr Freeman or Mr Turner might have incurred, and that was to ask the question: might they have negotiated more off the sale price if they had known of the defects? In other

1   Webb Resolutions Limited v E-Surv Limited [2012] All ER (D) 237.

words, knowing of defects gives you a negotiating tool and by not knowing of them you lose the chance to shave more off the price. This is known as "loss of chance", but it was not raised in the claim of Roger Jones Ltd.

The claim raised one other type of loss, for which Mr Turner alone had been compensated, and that was the return of his survey fee. Why had he been entitled to that back? He had received a survey report which, even if it was incomplete regarding the conservatory and the shower, was sufficient in every other respect. Rightly or wrongly, he had been compensated for the repairs. Why should he have got anything more? Imagine you engage a builder to install a new kitchen at a cost of £10,000 and he makes a mistake which later costs you £1,000 to put right. He owes you £1,000, but you do not get the original £10,000 back as well! Again, this is basic law, and the return of the survey fee was not a legitimate entitlement.

The defence would deny any loss had been incurred by Mr Freeman or Mr Turner.

Additional loss claimed by Roger Jones Ltd.

In relation to Mr Turner's complaint alone, Roger Jones Ltd. was claiming losses and costs over and above the cost of the repairs and the refund of the survey fee. These were the ombudsman's fee, Mr Turner's court fee of £70, administrative costs and expenses, interest and legal representative's costs. Before we look at these in turn, let us suppose, again for argument's sake, that John Smith had been negligent, that he had caused Mr Turner the cost of the repairs and that the law is such that the company was liable for those and the return of the survey fee, i.e. let us assume all my arguments to this point have been wrong. John Smith would be liable to Roger Jones Ltd. for the liability the company had owed to Mr Turner and nothing more. If there had been such a liability, it had been for the company to settle it quickly and, if it had not done so, that was not John Smith's fault or problem. If, on the other hand, the company had offered to settle the liability quickly, but Mr Turner had rejected that, whether mistakenly or unreasonably, so too that was not John Smith's fault or problem. A company must bear the cost of its own failures, and the cost of unreasonable or mistaken behaviour by clients is a normal business risk which companies bear on a daily basis. Neither the conduct of the company nor that of Mr Turner had been under the control of John Smith, and neither was his responsibility. With that in mind, it was difficult to see how John Smith could be responsible for losses additional to the cost of repairs and the survey fee.

The ombudsman's fee

If a client complains to the ombudsman, one of two things has happened – either the company has failed to promptly settle a legitimate liability to the client or the client is mistaken in his complaint. In either case, John Smith would not be liable. The former would be the fault of the company, and the second would not be John Smith's responsibility.

Before complaining to the ombudsman, Mr Turner had been offered £925 as a goodwill gesture by the company, being £500 for the conservatory repairs and £425 for the return of his survey fee. That offer was not an admission of liability. He had rejected it. At that time, John Smith had been willing to pay the £925.

When he complained to the ombudsman, Mr Turner had wanted the refund of his survey fee of £425; the cost of repairs to the conservatory, which at that time he stated as £650 (later in his court claim he would ask for £600); the cost of repairs to the shower, which he had said in an email had actually cost him £200 (in his later court claim he would ask for £354!); and, finally, the cost of repairs for fire damage to the roof of

£4,000 (another defect he had complained Mr Smith had not mentioned in his report; a complaint he would later abandon). The ombudsman chose not to interfere with the goodwill offer of £925 already made by Roger Jones Ltd. and ruled such sum be paid to Mr Turner. Nothing was awarded for the shower or the fire damage. In other words, Mr Turner's complaint to the ombudsman failed. It was an unjustified complaint. It achieved nothing over and above the amount the company (and John Smith) had already offered to pay. Why then should John Smith be responsible for the ombudsman's fee of £260?

The ombudsman's decision had no authority as a ruling on the true legal liability of the company, but had both parties accepted his resolution, a binding agreement would have been made. Mr Turner did not accept the resolution, just as he had not accepted the previous goodwill offer made by the company.

The fact the ombudsman upheld the goodwill offer of £925 did not mean the company was legally liable to Mr Turner for anything.

Mr Turner's court claim

Having rejected the company's offer and the ombudsman's resolution of £925, in the end, Mr Turner had issued a County Court claim against the company. By now, he was seeking the refund of his survey fee of £425, only £600 for the conservatory repairs, £354 for the shower repair and a court fee of £70.

The fact that Mr Turner had started court proceedings was not really of much interest to John Smith. The question was still what, if anything, had Mr Turner been entitled to from the company? Following my arguments above, whether as to negligence, causation or diminution in value, he was entitled to nothing. Even if all those arguments are wrong, at best he was entitled to £600 for the conservatory and £200 for the shower, a total of £800, since he was certainly not entitled to a refund of his survey fee and nor was he entitled to £354 for the shower when he had said in an email the repair had actually cost him £200. He had already been offered £925, which at an early stage Mr Smith had offered to pay. Was Mr Smith then to be at the mercy of whatever ongoing mischief Mr Turner was making for the company and at the mercy of how the company was deciding to deal with that? And what of the court fee? Since, at best, he was entitled to £800 for the cost of repairs but had rejected at the outset an offer of £925, no competent judge would have awarded him his court fee – he would have been sent away with a flea in his ear! Mr Turner's suit was unreasonable and mistaken in its entirety, yet the company paid him £1,250. He had not been entitled to anything. That payment might be explained on the basis of commercial convenience or goodwill, but those would be on the company's tab, not Mr Smith's.

Mr Turner's court claim could have been fought to the end, yet the company settled it. This settlement was irrelevant in deciding whether the company had been liable to Mr Turner for any amount. In the claim against John Smith, it was a red herring, as was the view expressed in the company's claim that the settlement "represented the best possible outcome that could reasonably be achieved". If the company had not been legally liable to Mr Turner for the settlement sum, it clearly had not been the best possible achievable outcome.

The words about this outcome being the best that could reasonably be achieved hint that the company's motive for settling had been that it was not worth the time and money to fight the claim. If that had been the reason for settling with Mr Turner, it was a business decision the company had to bear the cost of, and it was not something John Smith was liable for.

The company's claim also referred to the fact that solicitors provided by the company's insurers had recommended settlement of the claim. This was another red herring. It did not matter what those solicitors had advised. It would be for the judge dealing with the company's claim against John Smith to decide what liability, if any, the company had owed to Mr Turner. If the company had been badly advised by those solicitors, it should take it up with them and not with John Smith, who was not liable for any negligent advice by the company's solicitors!

Administrative costs and expenses

This assumed John Smith had left the company with a liability to Mr Turner which it had had to deal with and that these costs had not been occasioned by a mistaken or unreasonable pursuit by Mr Turner of his complaint or by failures or commercial decisions on the part of the company.

The costs and expenses were not specified in the company's claim and were said to be "not less than £100", so there was clearly an element of estimation going on. That did not matter if it was clear they must have been at least £100.

It would seem obvious that, if no liability had been owed to Mr Turner, the company was not going to recover anything from John Smith. In the end, Mr Turner had received £755 for repairs to the conservatory and shower. Even if the company had been liable to Mr Turner for the £755, at an early stage he had been offered £925, which John Smith had offered to pay. On any view, these administrative costs and expenses were incurred after the offer of £925, and they were clearly incurred because Mr Turner had unreasonably or mistakenly pursued his complaint. John Smith was surely not liable for those.

Interest

It is normal for a party to claim interest on any debt which is owed, but at that time 4% was normal and not the 8% claimed. The interest would be calculated on whatever amount it was decided was John Smith's liability, if any. Any dispute as to interest did not have to be included in the written defence as it was simply a matter for the judge at the end of the trial.

Legal representative's costs

These costs are fixed by regulations. If you instruct a lawyer to prepare your claim form, you can claim the fixed amount, which in this case was £80. However, these are not allowable if a defendant is sincere in his defence and the case goes to trial. Again, opposing these did not have to be included in the written defence.

The defence would deny liability for the ombudsman's fee, Mr Turner's court fee and the administrative costs and expenses.

Insurance

So far in considering the defence, the arguments have assumed Roger Jones Ltd. had been free to deny liability and dispute the complaints of Mr Freeman and Mr Turner without restriction. However, in the claim, there was mention of solicitors provided by the company's professional indemnity insurers. The role of the insurers had to be considered.

When insurers become involved with a policy claim, they normally take control, and the power to decide how to deal with a complaint against an insured company passes to them. In this case, if the insurers had taken control, a different argument would arise because Roger Jones Ltd. would argue that the company's loss was any payment they had had to make to the insurers under the policy excess, i.e. the company's loss would no longer be dependent on showing the company had been legally liable to the purchasers. The arguments as to causation, diminution in value, the refund of the survey fee, etc. would not be relevant. Even if the insurers had mistakenly agreed to compensate Mr Freeman and Mr Turner, or had done so for cost reasons, it would not matter. The argument would be that the company had had to comply with whatever decision the insurers had made and, providing they could establish negligence by John Smith (or a relevant contractual obligation owed by him), they had suffered loss, namely, whatever they had had to pay to the insurers under the policy excess.

Roger Jones Ltd's claim did not say the company's loss had been the result of the insurers taking control. The solicitors mentioned as having advised on Mr Turner's court claim appeared to have been provided under the legal expenses provision of the insurance, and that did not of itself mean the insurers had taken control of the complaint. Also, the sums involved in the two purchasers' claims had been well within the company's insurance policy excess, so it was likely the insurers had allowed Roger Jones Ltd. a free hand to decide whether or not to settle or fight the complaints. If Roger Jones Ltd. had been given a free hand (a fact that would have to be confirmed at trial), it would have to justify any payment to the purchasers by proving it had had a legal liability to compensate them. It would not be possible for it to say, "The insurers took over and we had no choice in the matter", and the insurance excess would be irrelevant.

Summary

The claim against John Smith, in essence, said he was at fault in not mentioning the defects, that Roger Jones Ltd. had had to compensate the purchasers and that John Smith now had to compensate the company.

Principally, the defence would be:

1. John Smith had not been at fault, but, if he had been,
2. that had not caused the purchasers any loss since they would have bought the houses even if they had known of the defects (the "but for" principle), and, in any event,
3. the correct measure of loss is diminution in value (not the cost of repairs), which was nil in both cases, and, in any event,
4. Mr Turner had not been entitled to a refund of his survey fee, and
5. the ombudsman's fee, Mr Turner's court fee and the administrative costs and expenses were caused by Mr Turner's mistaken or unreasonable pursuit of his complaint and/or a commercial decision by Roger Jones Ltd.

In a civil claim, to prove a fact, it is necessary to show it is more likely than not true. This standard of proof is known as the balance of probabilities. So, for example, when asking whether the shower was dripping at the time of the survey inspection, we have to ask: "On the evidence, is it more likely than not it was dripping?"

Having now read the defence arguments, has your opinion on John Smith's liability changed?

PRE-TRIAL

"Law is order and good law is good order."

Aristotle, *Politics*

Having set out their positions in the claim form and the written defence, the next stage was for the parties to fill out a simple form giving information which would assist a judge in giving procedural directions for an efficient trial. Amongst other things, the parties indicate how many witnesses they will have, whether or not they wish to rely on expert evidence and whether they think the case should be treated as a small claim. In the case of Roger Jones Ltd. v John Smith, there would be Messrs Jones and Smith giving evidence, neither party indicated there would be expert evidence and both parties agreed it was suitable to be treated as a small claim.

A district judge gave standard procedural directions to the effect that the parties had to send to one another and the court the documents which they would rely on at trial and a written statement from each witness. This had to be done no later than fourteen days prior to the trial, which the judge directed "should take no longer than ninety minutes".

The time restriction of ninety minutes was of concern since it did not seem possible that this case, involving allegations of professional negligence relating to two purchasers and three different defects, could be dealt with in ninety minutes or less. Although the hearing of a small claim can be informal, and the judge can break with the traditional form of a trial, the parties would still need to question the evidence, argue legal principles, make representations and receive the court's judgment; and though a matter worth £2,068.10 does not justify the same time and attention as a matter worth £200,000, there is still a basic requirement that any trial be fair, and the overriding objective of the governing rules is that cases be dealt with "justly and at proportionate cost". Further, Article 6 of the European Convention on Human Rights (incorporated into our laws by the Human Rights Act 1988) states, "... everyone is entitled to a fair and public hearing within a reasonable time by an independent and impartial tribunal established by law", and this includes a real opportunity to present their case or challenge the case against them. Perhaps the judge was of the view that the company's claim, for the reasons set out in the written defence, had little chance of success and the court would be able to promptly dispose of it!

The judge also invited the parties to take advantage of the court's mediation service, which is there to help the parties settle their differences and reach a compromise. John Smith declined that invitation since, on my advice, he believed his arguments to be strong and was not, therefore, minded to compromise. Further, since solicitors were advising the company and I was advising John Smith, I did not think a mediator would add anything to the communication already taking place.

In accordance with the judge's directions, the parties sent their documentation to the court and one another. This included the contract terms and conditions which Mr Freeman and Mr Turner had signed when ordering their surveys, the survey reports and, in the case of Mr Turner, correspondence between him and the company and documentation relating to his complaint to the ombudsman and his court action. It also included the witness statements of John Smith and Roger Jones.

Prior to the trial, I sent to the court and Borders Solicitors copies of relevant judgments of the higher courts. These dealt with the nature of a surveyor's duty, the "but for" principle, that diminution in value is the measure of any loss, that house valuations are not precise and the approach the court should take to the "loss of chance" argument (on which the company would later rely). It is a lawyer's duty to help ensure a court does not get the law wrong, and so it can be important to refer to previous, relevant and authoritative court decisions.

In a letter, Borders Solicitors agreed the correct measure of any loss suffered by Messrs Freeman and Turner was indeed diminution in value and not the cost of repairs (even though the claim form of Roger Jones Ltd. was clearly based on the cost of repairs and not diminution in value!). However, they claimed the two houses had diminished in value by the amount of the cost of repairs, i.e. by £150 in Mr Freeman's case and by £755 in Mr Turner's case.

Also prior to the trial, I prepared summaries of the defects with the two houses which John Smith had mentioned in his report. This I thought helpful because they were much shorter than the survey reports and they allowed the significance of the defects complained about to be seen in the context of all the defects which had been mentioned in the reports. The court could then ask questions relevant to the "loss of chance" and the "but for" principles, such as: "What difference would it have made if the defects complained about had been included in the reports?"; "Would Mr Freeman really have tried to get another £150 off the price, and might the seller have agreed to that (the house was already being sold at £5,000 less than the asking price)?"; and "In light of other defects with the house, would this £150 really have put Mr Freeman off buying the house?" Similar questions could be asked in the case of Mr Turner who, subsequent to the survey report, which valued the property at £348,000, even allowing for the defects mentioned in the report, had negotiated a price reduction to £340,000, an undervalue of £8,000. The court looking at the summary of the defects mentioned in the report could ask, "Would he really have been able to negotiate a further reduction because of the alleged defects to the conservatory and the shower?" I sent these summaries only to Borders Solicitors and not to the court since, in my view, it is wrong for a party to send to the court in advance of the trial anything which selectively emphasises only a part of the evidence which the court might consider. In any event, the summaries were merely a precis of the survey reports which had been sent to the court – the important thing was that Borders Solicitors was given the opportunity to complain about any inaccuracy with the summaries.

On the day of the trial, I was en route to collect John Smith, so we could travel to court together, when I received a call from the court advising me that the trial was not going to take place that day. The judge of the day, not being the judge who had given the earlier procedural directions, had decided the trial could not be dealt with in ninety minutes or less, and he changed the time estimate to three hours, which to my mind was still not enough time, but it was twice as good as ninety minutes!

So, essentially, what was the evidence the parties were going to rely on at trial?

1 Elm Close

There was little evidence relating to Mr Freeman's purchase. Principally, there was the standard HomeBuyer Report contract, the survey report and the invoice from the company that had treated the woodworm. However, there were no photographs showing the woodworm holes on the garage timbers, and the only evidence it had been "fairly extensive" was Roger Jones telling us so. John Smith had not at any stage been given an opportunity to see the woodworm evidence at the property.

The woodworm holes would still have been visible after being treated, so I contacted Mr Freeman asking if I could take photographs of them and explaining why, but he was happy with how Roger Jones Ltd. had dealt with his complaint and he did not want to do anything which would harm the company. He refused. I asked the company to indicate to Mr Freeman that it had no objections to my taking photographs, but it would not do so. So, basically, the company acted to prevent me examining key evidence. Would it then be just for the court to allow the company to proceed with its claim in so far as it related to 1 Elm Close? I intended to argue it would not be.

In saying the evidence of the woodworm at 1 Elm Close was fairly extensive in July and that it must have been visible to John Smith when he inspected the property the previous December, Roger Jones was giving expert evidence because such an assertion relies on expert knowledge of how woodworm behave. How else would he be able to explain why the problem could not have shown itself for the first time after John Smith inspected the property, namely, between December and the following July when it was reported to Roger Jones? Expert evidence cannot be given in a small claim trial without the permission of the judge, and Roger Jones Ltd. had said it was not relying on such evidence. That said, when the essence of the dispute in a case is the negligence of an expert surveyor, it is surely to be expected that the two surveyors giving evidence at trial, and who are the claimant and the defendant, will touch upon matters within their expertise. I had no objection to this evidence being given although, obviously, I would want to question Roger Jones about it, particularly since even a quick Internet search makes clear that woodworm holes are not entry holes but exit holes made when the woodworm rapidly break out of the wood in early summer, a fact consistent with the woodworm not having been visible to John Smith in December yet visible to Roger Jones the following July.

In his statement, John Smith simply said he had not seen any woodworm when he carried out his inspection.

5 Maple Avenue

There was more evidence in relation to Mr Turner's purchase. As with Mr Freeman, there were the HomeBuyer Report contract and the survey report.

In addition, there was documentation relating to the complaint to the ombudsman and to Mr Turner's eventual court claim. There were no invoices for any repair work carried out to the conservatory or the shower, but there was some interesting correspondence.

The correspondence suggested Mr Turner was a chancer. He had complained of fire damage to the main roof of the house, and he had sought £4,000 compensation for this in his complaint to the ombudsman, yet he later dropped that claim. Regarding the conservatory, he had initially said the roof needed replacing at a cost of between £8,000 and £12,000; then he said the repairs to the conservatory timbers, the shower and the fire-damaged roof had cost him "around £5,000" but he would "settle for half that"; later, he stated the conservatory timbers would cost "£600/700" to repair and the shower "cost £200 to repair", hence, he had sought £650 and £200 for the conservatory timbers and the shower, respectively, in his complaint to the ombudsman; he had claimed to have builders' quotations and "detailed costing", but none was produced, and none was available as evidence in the instant case; in his court claim, he had sued for a refund of his survey fee of £425, repairs to the conservatory timber of £600, repairs to the shower of £354 and his court fee of £70, giving a total of £1,449.

The correspondence also showed Roger Jones had written to Mr Turner rejecting his complaint and stating, "I will rigorously defend any allegations that we have not acted in a proper manner or in accordance with the RICS Standard Terms of Engagement". When writing to the ombudsman, Roger Jones had pointed out that the conservatory had been given a category 3 condition rating in the survey report, there had been no dripping from the shower unit at the time of John Smith's inspection and, in any event, a dripping shower "would not have been reported within the scope of a RICS HomeBuyer Survey and Valuation".

In his witness statement, Roger Jones explained Mr Turner had initially been made a goodwill offer by the company of £425, being the return of his survey fee, and then later £925, being the survey fee plus £500 for the conservatory. He said John Smith had been aware of the offers and had known he would need to pay. At one point, Mr Turner had sought a settlement of £2,500 and, Jones said, John Smith had offered to pay that, but he, Roger Jones, had refused to allow it. He said John Smith had told him that at the time of the survey his mind had not been fully on the job and he had had family problems. As to whether or not John Smith had been negligent, Jones said, "most certainly that was the case" regarding 1 Elm Close and, regarding 5 Maple Avenue, "there was clearly a merited claim to some extent… and such claim became settled and resolved upon the most favourable terms possible" upon the advice of solicitors.

Roger Jones also claimed in his statement that, had the two purchasers known of the defects prior to the purchase, they would have been able to negotiate a reduction in the price. He stated Mr Freeman would have been able to have secured a reduction of the £150 cost of the woodworm treatment.

Bizarrely, he then claimed Mr Turner would have been able to negotiate a reduction of, approximately, the £1,250 he had been paid by the company in settlement of his court action. Yet at the time when Mr Turner was buying the house, how could the settlement amount of a hypothetical future court action, based on facts which would have been fictitious and impossible (bear in mind this argument of the company contemplates the defects having been mentioned in the report and how the purchasers might have used that information to their advantage, whereas the court case was based on them not having been mentioned), influence the price the seller might accept? You have to imagine a Monty Python type of negotiation in which Mr Turner says to the house owner: "Now, I need you to use your imagination, but although my surveyor has told me of some defects to the conservatory and shower which will cost £755 to repair, if he had not done so, I would have complained, and a year from now I would have sued him, and he would then have paid me £1,250. So, I want you to reduce the sale price by £1,250 and not just by £755"! It is hard to believe such was drafted by a firm of solicitors. Anyway, this was the "loss of chance" argument, which I referred to in the previous chapter. It would need to be dealt with at the trial.

In his statement, John Smith explained the shower had not been dripping, he had adequately covered the defects with the conservatory in his report and, in any event, he had met Mr Turner at the property on the day of his inspection and told him the conservatory roof was in poor repair and would be expensive to fix. He accepted he had offered to pay compensation, but that was not because he had done anything wrong.

It is worth noting that at no stage did Roger Jones inspect 5 Maple Avenue. It follows, the only evidence the shower had been in disrepair came from Mr Turner, a man who appeared to be untrustworthy and was not going to be a witness.

Pre-trial concerns

In considering Mr Smith's chances at trial, I had only two concerns regarding 1 Elm Close. Firstly, had the insurance company taken control (giving Roger Jones no say in the matter) and decided to settle? That seemed unlikely, but it needed to be confirmed. Secondly, there was the issue of "loss of chance". Of course, I would also challenge Roger Jones on his assertion that the woodworm had been there, and visible, when John Smith inspected the property, but, even if I lost that point, provided I could deal with the insurance and "loss of chance" issues, it did not really matter as it seemed to me unarguable that there had been no causation (the "but for" principle) not to mention diminution in value.

Regarding 5 Maple Avenue, I had three concerns. Firstly, there was the issue of whether the insurers had taken control. The correspondence suggested that had not happened, but I needed to confirm it. Secondly, John Smith had offered to pay compensation at different points – had a binding agreement in that regard been made between John Smith and the company? None of John Smith's offers had been accepted and John Smith had not been a party to the compensation figure eventually agreed with Mr Turner, yet that was the figure the company was claiming from John Smith – why would they do that if there already existed an agreement that John Smith would pay a certain amount? There appeared to be no agreement, but I needed to confirm that also. Thirdly, there was the issue of "loss of chance". Yes, I would deal with the arguments that the shower had not been dripping and the conservatory defects had been adequately dealt with in the survey report etc., but, again, provided I put to bed my three concerns, I was not at all concerned as it seemed to me unarguable that there had been no causation let alone diminution in value.

"Loss of chance"

As I have explained, this is the notion that, in a case such as this, by not knowing of defects not mentioned in a survey report, a purchaser loses the chance to negotiate a lower price for the property. It is an argument that does not arise until it is proven defects have not been mentioned when they should have been. So, I had to imagine the judge at trial would find, more likely than not, that the woodworm had been visible to John Smith and/or the shower had been dripping, and that one or both of these and/or the rotten conservatory timber, ought to have been mentioned in the survey reports. The law which deals with "loss of chance" would then pose the following questions:

If the defects had been mentioned in the reports –

1. Was it more likely than not the purchasers would have tried to negotiate a price reduction from the seller?
2. Was it more likely than not there would have been a real (and not merely a speculative) possibility that those negotiations would have been partly or wholly successful?
3. If "yes" to 1. and 2. above, what valuation should be given to that possibility[1]?

So, by way of example, let us suppose it was crystal clear both that Mr Turner would have tried to negotiate a further price discount and that the seller would have been prepared to agree to a reduction. The court would ask how likely it had been that he would have got a reduction of the full amount of the repairs. If the court were to think there had been a 50% chance Mr Turner would have got a reduction of £800, his loss would be set at £400 – that is what 3. means.

---

1   Allied Maples Group Ltd. v Simmons & Simmons (a firm) [1995] 4 All ER 907.

Neither Mr Freeman nor Mr Turner was going to give evidence at the trial, and nor were the sellers, about whom we knew nothing. How then could Roger Jones Ltd. prove 1. and 2. above? Would Mr Freeman have bothered to try to get a reduction of £150? If he had, would the seller have been amenable since he was already selling at £5,000 less than the asking price? What had been the seller's financial situation, and would it have permitted a further price reduction? Similar questions arose in the case of Mr Turner who was already buying at an £8,000 discount to the offer the seller had initially accepted from him and John Smith's valuation (though still £15,000 above the initial asking price). There simply was not enough information for these questions to be answered, and I felt confident I could defeat the "loss of chance" argument on points 1. and 2. in relation to both Mr Freeman and Mr Turner.

Approaching the trial, I believed John Smith had every reason to feel confident. What do you think?

THE TRIAL

"Of all injustice, that is the greatest
which goes under the name of law."

Roger L'Estrange (attributed to)

An inauspicious start

On the day of the trial in February 2015, Roger Jones attended
with a barrister, Miss Brown, and I accompanied John Smith.
What bad luck for my friend to find that the district judge
was the original judge whose time limit for the trial of ninety
minutes had been changed by the later judge to three hours due
to the amount of case documentation. Well, authority does not
like to be contradicted, and just who was it that had troubled the
court with the majority of that documentation (that is to say,
evidence and law), including case reports from the higher courts
which, God forbid, actually suggested that points of law would
be raised during the trial? Er, that was me! Here was a judge who
clearly did not want to spend much time dealing with the case

and whose decision I had caused to be altered, and there was I having indicated in advance to the court that, actually, there was quite a bit of evidence and law to be considered, a fact which was inconsistent with the judge's ability to deal with the case quickly. How would she react? Would she give priority to the evidence, the law and justice or to the clock?

Whatever the reason, I received a very frosty reception from the judge in stark contrast to that given to Miss Brown. Dressed in a suit and tie and looking just as I did when I had been a practising solicitor, I was met with a steely, hostile stare and the opening words, "And you are?". You will note the absence of the word "sir". I stated my name and the judge recognised it for, as I have said, I had written several times to the court forwarding documentation, indicating who I was and that, now retired and not a practising solicitor, I would be representing John Smith at his trial as a lay representative. Given the judge had recognised my name, she would surely have known all this and exactly who I was.

A lay representative is someone who is not a lawyer but is allowed to represent a party at a small claim hearing. This right is given by the Lay Representatives (Right of Audience) Order 1999 and is confirmed in paragraph 3.2 of Practice Direction 27 (Small Claims Track), which accompanies Rule 27 of the Civil Procedure Rules. It is very unlikely the judge would not have known this.

The judge then announced she believed I was there as a "McKenzie friend". This is a legal term for a person who is not there to represent a party by speaking on his behalf but is there to assist a party who is representing himself. I explained I was there to act as a lay representative for Mr Smith, for which I received the first of many scowls. She confirmed she had seen that in the correspondence. Why then had she tried to limit me to being a McKenzie friend? She asked Miss Brown if she had any objections (she had none). That also seemed odd to me since there could not have been any objections – to use a lay representative is a right given to a party to a small claim. It was crystal clear the judge did not want me to represent Mr Smith.

The judge asked if the parties had reached any settlement and, upon being told they had not, another scowl headed in my direction alone. The judge was told by Miss Brown that the dispute remained that which had been set out in the claim form and the written defence.

From the judge's opening manner and comments, Mr Smith and I would later tell one another we knew we were in trouble even before the trial had started. The judge had clearly taken a dislike to me based on my correspondence with the court. She had the air of someone who had already decided who was going to win, and who was going to lose, this trial.

The claimant's opening

At the beginning of a civil trial, the claimant's lawyer addresses the judge, and the defendant does not at that stage reply. Accordingly, Miss Brown addressed the judge. She told her there were three key points: firstly, whether Mr Smith had agreed he would pay any costs incurred by the company as a result of his work; secondly, whether the company had been right to make the payments to Mr Freeman and Mr Turner, which she said involved asking whether Mr Smith had been negligent and whether the payments had been made to limit the loss to the company; thirdly, was any loss measured as diminution in value or not. She asserted that Mr Smith had been negligent and "the most sensible commercial decision" to take in an attempt to limit losses had been to make the payments to the purchasers. This reduction of the arguments in the claim form and the written defence suited Miss Brown's purpose, and she cannot be criticised for that, but let us pause a moment and have a closer look.

The first point proposed by Miss Brown (had Mr Smith agreed he would pay any costs incurred by the company as a result of his work?) was, with the possible exception of the ombudsman's fee, irrelevant, and such an agreement was certainly not asserted in the claim form. Even if Mr Smith had agreed to pay costs associated with his work, those would not encompass compensation payable to a client due to negligence or consequential costs incurred by the company. Costs associated with his engagement would encompass such things as professional fees, insurance, stationery, secretarial support, vehicle use, etc. If the court were to find John Smith to have been negligent, costs to the company caused by such would be considered, but that would not be the result of any agreement by Mr Smith to pay costs. The court should ask: had there been negligence and, if so, what loss did that cause to the company having regard to any legal liability owed to each purchaser? Whilst the ombudsman's fee was capable of being considered a general cost associated with Mr Smith's engagement, clear evidence would be needed (in my view, in writing) as to what the parties had agreed in that regard. Although she had not specified them, the costs to which Miss Brown was referring could not have been (the ombudsman's fee excepted) costs associated with, and naturally flowing from, Mr Smith's engagement by the company. Rather, they were costs resulting from legal claims made against the company by the two purchasers.

The second point proposed by Miss Brown (had the company been right to make the payments to Mr Freeman and Mr Turner, i.e. in her words, had Mr Smith been negligent, and had the payments been made to limit the loss to the company?), mentioned negligence and loss, and implicit within those (though she did not draw attention to them) were the issues of causation and what kinds of loss had been incurred by the purchasers and, hence, by the company. Talking of limiting loss, she had introduced the legal concept of mitigation of loss, which places an obligation on an injured party to take all reasonable steps to hold their loss to a minimum. In the context of this case, she could only have meant that if the payments had not been made to Mr Freeman and Mr Turner when they were, the losses incurred by the company would have increased, but this would not justify the company having paid compensation if no legal liability had existed, for in such circumstances there would have been no loss to mitigate. Prima facie, Mr Smith owed a liability to Roger Jones Ltd. only if his actions had left the company with a liability to the two house-purchasers. It was important to ask what had caused any loss to the company – had it been an unreasonable or mistaken complaint by a client, a failure by the company to deal with a complaint properly or a mistake by Mr Smith? Really, it was Miss Brown's comment that the compensation had been the most sensible commercial decision which was behind her assertion of limiting the loss. Effectively, she was saying if Mr Smith had been negligent, the company had been entitled to sort it out according to its commercial interests. Such an argument does not hold water since even if Mr Smith had been negligent, that did not mean the house-purchasers had suffered any claimable loss, for it is necessary to consider causation (e.g. the "but for" principle) and what kind of loss is relevant (i.e. cost of repairs or diminution in value). It would not be acceptable for a company to say: "Legally we weren't liable to pay anything to the clients, but it was cheaper for us to pay than fight, and now you must pay us"! What would you say if a company you had done work for said that to you?

Miss Brown's third point (should loss be measured as diminution in value or not?) was satisfactory in part, but it did not cover such things as the ombudsman's fee or the survey fee. Also, the issue of measuring loss would only arise once it was established that some loss had been caused by any negligence, i.e. that the purchasers would not have bought their houses at the prices they had paid if Mr Smith had included the defects complained of in his reports.

You may have noticed Miss Brown's three points are not obviously consistent with each other. On the one hand, she seemed to be claiming the compensation paid to the purchasers was a cost and Mr Smith was party to an agreement to pay costs associated with his work; on the other hand, she was arguing Mr Smith had been negligent and the company had acted reasonably in paying compensation. Well, if her first point was right, why in her second point was it necessary to show negligence or that the company had acted reasonably? Vice versa, if Mr Smith had been negligent, why would it be necessary to prove an agreement to pay costs? In effect, Miss Brown seemed to be saying she was relying on point one (an agreement to pay costs) but, if that was incorrect, she was relying on point two (negligence by John Smith). They were alternatives for the judge to consider. Her third point dealt with a legal question, that of how damages were to be measured in assessing compensation payable to the clients. The fact she considered that to be relevant meant she also considered relevant the whole issue as to whether the company had owed any legal liability to the clients (otherwise, it would not be necessary to consider how any loss to them was to be measured!). That would necessarily involve looking at causation (the "but for" principle) and the exact nature and extent of the liability to the clients (e.g. the survey fee). Miss Brown did not explain why she thought the legal liability to the clients was relevant. After all, following the logic of her arguments, if Mr Smith was liable under an agreement to pay costs, or because he had been at fault and the company had correctly paid to limit its loss through a sensible commercial decision, why would there need to be anything legally owed to the clients? It would be enough, would it not, that a client pursued a complaint whether mistakenly or not? Of course, it might be argued some of the company's claimed losses were recoverable subject to an agreement to pay costs (point one) and others on the basis the company had acted reasonably following negligence by Mr Smith (point two), and the nature and extent of the liability owed by the company to the client (point three) was relevant to whether the company had acted reasonably (within point two), but none of this was set out by Miss Brown, and the judge would have to make it very clear if she were to base her decision on such reasoning, otherwise, the logic and consistency would not be apparent. Even if the three points were brought together in a logical fashion, they were the wrong approach and highly unlikely to deliver a correct and just decision.

I will now set out, with commentary, a summary of the evidence given at the trial in the order in which it occurred.

Roger Jones's evidence-in-chief

As is normal practice, the claimant's written statement was admitted as evidence, and this was supplemented by some questioning from Miss Brown who followed the three points which she had set out in her opening speech.

Regarding her first point, that of an agreement to pay costs, Mr Jones stated that, when he had engaged Mr Smith to do work for his firm, Mr Smith had agreed to pay any additional costs incurred by the company as a result of the relationship, including in his, Mr Jones's, mind, "having to pay out any damages"!

Now I ask you, is it usual for people to agree to pay for damages when they are contracting to do work for a company, or is this an example of a witness saying what he thought needed to be said to win his case? In any event, it is liability that determines whether or not you pay damages. If you are not liable, you do not pay damages and, if you are, you do – no agreement is necessary.

Mr Jones also said Mr Smith had agreed to pay any insurance excess on any claim arising out of an error on his part.

Well, that would only be relevant if the insurance company had taken control of the claims and the decision-making had been out of Mr Jones's hands. If Mr Jones had had the power to decide whether to settle or dispute the claims he would, clearly, have to justify any decision to settle if he wanted reimbursement from Mr Smith, and that justification would have to be such that it showed why Mr Smith was legally liable to reimburse the company.

Regarding her second point, negligence and limiting loss to the company, Mr Jones stated he had not inspected Mr Turner's property, but £925 had been offered to Mr Turner as compensation, which Mr Smith had been willing to pay. He then explained Mr Turner had referred the matter to the ombudsman, who upheld the £925 offered and that, subsequently, Mr Turner had issued the court proceedings which, on the advice of solicitors, had been settled in the sum of £1,250, by which time Mr Smith was no longer involved in the matter.

None of that determined whether Mr Smith had left the company legally liable to Mr Turner.

It might be said that if Mr Smith had offered to pay the £925, it was an admission of guilt on his part, but that would not be enough to make him liable, because if the evidence as a whole showed he was not liable, any belief on his part that he was would simply be mistaken and of no consequence. Just as a person can deny guilt and be found guilty, so a person can admit guilt and be found innocent – one can be mistaken in either direction. Suppose Mr Smith thought that in his report for Mr Turner he should have included the defects complained of and, therefore, that he had breached his duty; that still left the arguments as to causation, what losses had been incurred and how loss should be measured – legal issues likely to be beyond Mr Smith's knowledge. Also, the offer of £925 had been for the defects in the conservatory and the return of the survey fee, and it did not encompass the shower, so, at most, Mr Smith might be taken to have admitted breaching his duty regarding the conservatory defects. Offering the return of the survey fee did not reflect any legal liability since, as a matter of law, Mr Turner was most definitely not entitled to the return of that fee.

I have dealt previously[1] with the issue of the ombudsman's fee. The ombudsman's report was, surprisingly, not produced by Roger Jones Ltd. at the trial, and the evidence before the court from the ombudsman's office did not show whether the ombudsman thought Mr Smith had been at fault. Even if it had, and if such evidence had been admissible as to whether Mr Smith had been negligent (it would constitute expert opinion evidence and, strictly speaking, permission from the judge would be needed to admit it for that purpose), it would not have helped with the issues of causation, what losses had been incurred or how loss should be measured (issues on which the ombudsman's opinion would not be admissible and which involved questions of law outside his expertise), but, rather, it would only have gone to whether Mr Smith should have included the defects in the report.

As previously mentioned[2], when there is a dispute, an offer by someone becomes binding if accepted by the other party; it becomes an enforceable agreement. Mr Turner had not accepted the offer of £925 from the company, and so the offer had lapsed. The company had not accepted any offer from Mr Smith in any way that was binding, as evidenced by the fact it had felt free later to ask Mr Smith for the amount eventually paid out to Mr Turner, an amount Mr Smith had never offered and which had not been discussed with him. Had there been a binding agreement that Mr Smith would pay the company £925 in settlement of his part in the dispute, the company would not later have asked him for £1,250. It is also the law that a counter-offer destroys an offer, so the company's request for £1,250 destroyed any offer previously

---

1   See "The ombudsman's fee" in the Defence chapter.
2   See "Pre-trial concerns" in the Pre-trial chapter.

made by Mr Smith. In other words, notwithstanding any offer he had made, there was no binding agreement between Mr Smith and the company that he would pay anything in settlement of Mr Turner's complaint.

Again[3], the spectre of the company having received advice from solicitors had raised its head. Mr Jones was saying it had been reasonable to pay the £1,250 because the solicitors had so advised, and, therefore, Mr Smith should reimburse the company. Piffle! The solicitors' advice did not determine whether the company was liable to Mr Turner; this would be for the judge to decide, and the solicitors' opinion was irrelevant and inadmissible. Expert opinion on the law is inadmissible since such is for the judge alone to decide. Had Mr Smith chosen these solicitors? Had he been privy to the discussions with them or their advice? If they had given bad advice, the company had best take it up with them and not with Mr Smith! The fact the company had acted on solicitors' advice was being used to spuriously feed the notion that, if the company showed it had dealt with Mr Turner's claim reasonably, Mr Smith should be liable even if the company had owed no legal liability to Mr Turner. Arguments were being put that it had been reasonable for the company to act on legal advice and to pay Mr Turner rather than to spend time and money fighting his claim. This notion of acting reasonably is not the legal test. If, in a case such as this, you want to recover your payment in court from the likes of Mr Smith, you have to have paid a Mr Freeman or a Mr Turner because you were liable to them, not because it was reasonable to do so. Mr Smith was entitled to say to the company it had owed no liability to Mr Turner, it should have resisted his claim and, if the company had chosen not to do so, that was no business of his but, rather, it had been a commercial decision by the company in dealing with a mistaken claim by a client. Why should Mr Smith pick up the tab for Mr Turner's mistaken and unreasonable complaint when, clearly (if nothing else, applying the "but for" principle), the man

---

3   See "Mr Turner's court claim" in the Defence chapter.

had been entitled to nothing, yet he had rejected £925, which Mr Smith had been willing to pay! The folly of the argument that the company had acted reasonably by relying on legal advice and, somehow, that justified Mr Smith reimbursing the company, demonstrates very well why the test was not whether the company acted reasonably – it will always be reasonable to act on legal advice, but it is absolutely not the law of our land that a Mr Smith would thereby be liable for negligent advice by the solicitors! Hence, we can conclude, reasonableness is not the test. And just as Mr Smith was not liable for the quality of any legal advice the company received, so too he was not responsible for mistake and unreasonableness on Mr Turner's part, no matter how reasonably the company had acted in light of it.

Regarding Mr Freeman's claim, Mr Jones stated he had inspected the garage timbers, which had fairly extensive woodworm and any surveyor should have alerted the client to it.

So, as a surveyor, he was giving expert evidence about what would be competent in such circumstances, but he was also giving expert evidence about how woodworm behave because from other evidence it was clear he inspected the property seven months after Mr Smith. He was saying that all those months earlier the woodworm evidence would have been visible and should have been seen by Mr Smith, and, to say that, he had to be able to explain why the woodworm evidence could not have shown itself for the first time a day, a week, a month or several months after Mr Smith's inspection, and, to do that, he had to have expert knowledge of how woodworm behave.

Cross-examination of Roger Jones

Mr Jones said he would not have expected reimbursement from Mr Smith if he had not been negligent.

How then was the money claimed by the company a cost associated with Mr Smith's engagement (Miss Brown's point one)? Such a cost does not generally depend upon there having been negligence. A contract might draft a clause to deal with costs payable in the event of negligence, but it would need to be carefully worded and in writing (unless there was no dispute between the parties as to what had been verbally agreed). Apart from Mr Jones's claim that, "in his mind", Mr Smith had agreed to pay damages as a cost, in this case there had been no suggestion there had been any discussion, let alone agreement, as to what costs would be payable in the event of negligence by Mr Smith – not in the claim form, not in Miss Brown's opening speech, not in Mr Jones's written statement, not in Mr Jones's oral evidence and not in any documentary evidence. Reimbursement of any loss incurred by the company was clearly not owed by Mr Smith under any agreement to pay costs.

Mr Jones confirmed, in relation to both Mr Freeman's and Mr Turner's claims, the insurance company had allowed the company to decide whether or not to settle or fight the claims.

Bingo! Any argument about having to pay the insurance excess had just gone. Mr Jones would have to justify why the company had chosen to pay compensation to the two house-purchasers. He would have to show that Mr Smith had left the company legally obliged to compensate Mr Freeman and Mr Turner, and there should be none of this nonsense that paying was the reasonable thing to do, the commercially cost-effective option or good customer relations.

I then referred Mr Jones to the contract which Mr Freeman and Mr Turner had signed instructing Roger Jones Ltd. to prepare a survey report. The contract was of great importance in understanding exactly what the duty of Mr Smith had been when he prepared his reports.

The contract stated one of the objectives of the survey report was to ensure the purchaser paid a reasonable price for the house. Mr Jones accepted both Mr Freeman and Mr Turner had paid a reasonable price for their property.

The contract also stated as an objective that the survey report should mention any serious or urgent defects or specific risks with the property.

Turning, specifically, to the issue of negligence regarding the woodworm in Mr Freeman's garage, Mr Jones accepted Mr Smith had not been given an opportunity to inspect it; that he, Mr Jones, had not taken any photos of it; that the visible evidence of the woodworm would still be there; and that he had declined to give consent to my going to take photos of it! The complaint from Mr Freeman had been received in July, some seven months after Mr Smith had surveyed the property in December. He accepted the holes in wood which evidence woodworm are not made when the woodworm enter, but are made when they exit the wood. He accepted the holes he had seen had led him to believe the woodworm had been active at that time. When I put to him "active" meant fresh and recent, he replied, "possibly". He continued to maintain there were too many holes for them all to have come out since December. I then put to him that a large number of the holes could have come out since December, to which he replied, "I'm not an expert on it, I don't know", but he accepted it was possible.

So, his evidence that the woodworm holes would have been visible to Mr Smith depended on an expertise he was saying he did not have! On the one hand, he was saying there were too many holes for them all to have come out since December but, on the other hand, he was not really expert enough to know. Cripes!

Turning to the issue of negligence regarding Mr Turner's property, when I put to him there had been no serious or urgent defect or specific risk, Mr Jones said the rotting beam in the conservatory had been "pretty serious" and should have been mentioned. I pointed out to him he had written to Mr Turner stating he had been satisfied the survey had been carried out in a proper manner and he would rigorously defend any allegations to the contrary. He justified that letter on the basis that insurers require a company should not admit liability and the letter was written to "reduce or get rid of the claim".

In other words, he was saying his letter was a lie. Note also, he was not saying the alleged dripping shower should have been mentioned.

Mr Jones accepted there was a difference between a Building Survey and a HomeBuyer Report and that, with the latter, the purchaser did not get a detailed report but, rather, the condition of the property was dealt with by pointing out defects which affected its value. He accepted the surveyor had discretion as to what the important issues were, and which defects were serious, and minor matters that did not affect the value of the property would generally not be included. He accepted the financial duty owed by a surveyor to a purchaser was to ensure they did not overpay for the property. He also accepted neither Mr Freeman nor Mr Turner had overpaid.

So, on the one hand, Mr Jones was saying the defects in Mr Turner's conservatory should have been mentioned in his survey report (in stark contradiction to the letter he had written to Mr Turner) and the woodworm mentioned in Mr Freeman's report, but, on the other hand, he was accepting Mr Smith had complied with his financial duty to both purchasers. How then had they suffered any financial loss?

I then turned to the issues of causation and "loss of chance" regarding Mr Freeman's purchase. Mr Jones accepted it was unlikely Mr Freeman would have pulled out of the purchase because of £150 of woodworm treatment and that it was not known whether the vendor would have reduced the purchase price if evidence of woodworm had been brought to his attention.

Returning to Mr Turner, I asked Mr Jones if he thought him trustworthy. He responded, "How do you define trustworthy? He was challenging."

Now I ask you, does "trustworthy" need to be defined, or was Mr Jones trying to avoid answering a question he did not like?

He went on to agree that Mr Turner was "pretty sharp" but then said he was not sure he was sharp and thought he was just "determined".

The character of Mr Turner was relevant because his word alone (not given as a witness in this trial) was the only evidence the shower had been dripping.

I mentioned earlier[4] that, prior to the trial, I had prepared a document which set out all the defects mentioned by Mr Smith in his survey report prepared for Mr Turner. This had been sent to Borders Solicitors so they could dispute its accuracy, which they did not do. This short document, a significant reduction of the survey report, allowing the court readily to see the defects mentioned, would have allowed the court to judge the relative importance of the defects which Mr Turner complained had not been mentioned. This was particularly relevant to the issue of "loss of chance" since the survey report had mentioned numerous defects (including the condition 3 rating for the conservatory), and Mr Turner had managed to reduce his original offer of £348,000, which the vendor had originally accepted, to £340,000, and this fell to be considered against an asking price of £325,000. If the report had mentioned the specifics of the rotten timber in the conservatory and the dripping shower, would Mr Turner have tried to negotiate the price down further, and would the vendor have entertained such an attempt? Seeing all the defects identified in the report would, with the "but for" principle in mind, also allow the court to judge whether Mr Turner would have been put off his purchase by any defects not mentioned.

Earlier[5], I also said that, prior to the trial, the judge had given a procedural direction that any document to be relied

---

4   See the Pre-trial chapter.
5   See the Pre-trial chapter.

on at trial had to be sent to the court and the other party in advance. As I explained, I decided not to send to the court my document setting out the defects. Firstly, these defects were contained in the survey report which the court and the claimant had. Secondly, my document was highlighting only part of the relevant evidence and, in my opinion, that should only be done at trial (otherwise, it could be alleged I was trying to influence the judge before the trial by emphasising evidence which I had cherry-picked). Thirdly, the document had been sent to the claimant company so that it could voice any disagreement ahead of the trial, and it had not done so. However, when I tried to refer to this document, the judge was not amused.

The judge had interrupted me prior to this (for example, she had questioned whether I could cross-examine Mr Jones as an expert on the behaviour of woodworm), her manner supercilious. I had ridden her icy stares, and she had looked at the wall clock frequently, but now she seemed to lose her self-control and bawled at me as if I were a naughty schoolboy and she a Victorian schoolmistress. Suffice it to say, when I tried to present her with the summary of the defects, she objected to my not having sent this document to the court prior to the trial. Miss Brown actually spoke up for me, telling the judge the document did not add anything by way of evidence and that it simply extracted parts from evidence which had been sent to the court. The judge then revealed her real concern, a matter that had been foremost in her mind back when she had said the trial should only last ninety minutes – the clock! She said she wanted us to focus on how much time we had and that she was conscious of my detailed cross-examination. She asked me to keep my eye closely on the clock so we could "get through it" if I had many more questions to ask. She told me to focus on the issues I wished to ask about (was I likely to do anything else?). She then said something even more extraordinary…

She said she had "seen" there were three issues which had been raised by the claimant as outstanding in the case, and those issues related to a contract, whether the claimant was correct in paying the householders and quantum (the legal word for the amount of any compensation). She asked that everyone focus on those three issues. Of course, she had not "seen" those issues anywhere. They were not all set out in the claim form; and there were other highly relevant issues set out in the written defence. She had merely heard them from Miss Brown in her opening speech and was accepting them as the case issues. She was not having regard to the arguments in the written defence which I had filed, and she had not yet heard me make any reply to Miss Brown's opening speech. Well, last I looked, both parties to a trial have a say as to what the issues are, and it was extremely concerning that this judge was uncritically accepting the version put forward by Miss Brown. When I tried to respond, the judge cut me off immediately and, again, said she wanted me to be conscious of time. She said she was affording me "this" (I still do not know quite what she was affording me) because I was a solicitor, "albeit a retired solicitor" who was there in "a quasi, if I may say, professional role". Well, it really does not matter who you are or what your title is. What matters is how you conduct yourself and the quality of what you say. I confirmed I was there only as a lay representative, to which she again replied that she wanted me to be conscious of the time and told me I had fifteen minutes in which to finish my cross-examination! So, no matter that relevant issues and evidence would not be properly considered, this judge wanted this trial over with quickly. Furthermore, she appeared biased in favour of Miss Brown, yet her judge's oath required she act "without fear or favour, affection or ill will". I had been concerned about this judge from the very beginning, and my task now felt like a suicide mission.

What was I to do? Judges in a small claim trial have a wide discretion to control how a trial is conducted, including how much time is given to each issue and the evidence, and even the form the trial takes, which might range from the traditional witness being subjected to cross-examination to a casual discussion with the witnesses and the representatives with the judge asking relevant questions. There are of course rules to be followed, and where the judge has the power to disapply them she must be ready to explain why. Above all, the judge must try to achieve justice and, as mentioned earlier, the European Convention on Human Rights makes it obligatory that each party should have an opportunity to present its case or challenge the case against it. It seemed to me the judge was biased and not interested in ensuring that all relevant issues and evidence be considered. She had wanted the trial to last no more than ninety minutes, but it had since been allocated three hours. In truth, it needed more than that, and the judge could have allowed more time if she had wished. The obligation was hers to ensure justice was done. I could have asked for an adjournment, but the trial had already been adjourned once and, having started, it was easier for it to continue for as long as was reasonably required. This judge was not going to grant an adjournment. I could have told the judge of my concerns that she was biased, that she was more interested in time than justice and that she was not allowing me to deal with highly relevant matters, but that would have antagonised her further and, I have no doubt, made matters even worse for Mr Smith. Such a complaint would have laid the basis for a subsequent appeal, but my experience is the higher courts are unlikely to allow appeals on that basis. It was unlikely Mr Smith would want to appeal to the European Court of Human Rights, which would require exhausting all possible appeals within this country first. Making any complaint would also have eaten into the precious time this judge was going to allow me. I was confident the evidence was coming out favourably for Mr Smith and I could tease out enough to make it legally impossible for the judge to find in favour of the claimant.

I might have to cut corners and abandon some of the issues, but if the judge ignored the obvious, we would be able to appeal her mistakes. I decided to stick to the evidence and the law and to ride the judge's unpleasantness.

Returning to my questioning of Mr Jones, he agreed an expert was not needed for a dripping shower to be noted, and he was unable to say the shower had been dripping at the time Mr Smith inspected the property. He believed an invoice had been produced when Mr Turner was suing the company, and he thought a video had at some point been sent, but he had not seen it.

Neither the invoice nor the video was before the court, and nor had they been sent to Mr Smith – this was the first mention of them! There was, however, before the court an email from Mr Turner expressly stating it had cost £200 to fix the shower so, clearly, no more than that could possibly be considered as valid.

He agreed there had been no binding agreement between the company and Mr Smith that the latter would pay a specific sum in compensation to Mr Turner.

This meant, therefore, Mr Smith had been free to change his mind about paying £925 or any other amount.

He accepted he knew nothing about the vendors.

This was relevant to the "loss of chance" issue.

I put it to him that had Mr Turner known of the defects of which he had complained, he would not have been put off buying the house since to do so would have meant writing off solicitors' fees, the survey fee and other costs. He accepted Mr Turner had been "pretty determined to buy the house whatever".

Bingo again! As with his answer regarding Mr Freeman's purchase, the "but for" principle meant this was fatal to any argument that the company had had any liability to compensate Mr Turner. They had owed him nothing.

Restricted and hurried by the judge, I had to leave my cross-examination there. Still, I believed I had drawn out of Mr Jones the answers needed to put to bed the two outstanding concerns

I had had before the trial relating to Mr Freeman's complaint (the insurers having control and "loss of chance") and the three outstanding concerns I had had before the trial relating to Mr Turner's complaint (the insurers having control, an agreement that Mr Smith would pay a specific sum and "loss of chance"), and the evidence wholly supported the dismissal of the claim in its entirety since the effect of the "but for" principle was unarguable. Yet there was this judge!

Re-examination of Roger Jones

Here, Miss Brown drew out of Mr Jones that, regarding Mr Turner's survey report, he had formed the view "very early on" that Mr Smith had been negligent since the rotten beams were not noted and should have been, which, he said, was borne out by the ombudsman's report, which, he said, stated the survey report should have been more specific.

Although there was some documentation before the court relating to the ombudsman's involvement, a report saying Mr Smith's survey report should have been more specific was not. Why was it not, and why had the defence not been sent a copy? The judge didn't shout at anyone for that! Note again, the allegedly dripping shower was noticeably absent in this exchange (as indeed it had been in the ombudsman's determination).

The judge asked Mr Jones to explain the difference between a Building Survey and a HomeBuyer Report. Mr Jones confirmed a Building Survey would be much more detailed and would not usually include a valuation.

The judge then asked him if it was his evidence that the defects which were the subject of the trial would have been noted regardless of whether it was a Building Survey or a HomeBuyer Report, to which he replied, "certainly".

There's nothing quite like a leading question from the judge! For me, this was further confirmation of the judge's bias. She knew the answer she wanted, and she knew the answer she would get. Was she laying the groundwork so she could give the judgment she wanted to give?

John Smith's evidence-in-chief

Mr Smith's signed witness statement was admitted as his evidence-in-chief.

Cross-examination of John Smith

Miss Brown began by asking Mr Smith about the company's professional indemnity insurance policy. Mr Smith explained he had been named on the policy and he had contributed to the cost of the premium. He denied he would have been responsible for any excess payable on the insurance in the event of any claim, even a big one.

Mr Smith claimed he had sufficiently dealt with the conservatory defects at Mr Turner's house by giving the conservatory a condition 3 rating, which was like a "red alert".

Mr Smith agreed he had offered to pay compensation to Mr Turner to settle his complaint. Miss Brown asked him why he had done that if he had been paying for his insurance and had not expected to pay towards any claim against the company. He said it was to stop the claim progressing, and he had wanted at that time just to clear the matter to prevent a protracted case. Miss Brown put to him he had offered to pay because he had been accepting responsibility, specifically, for the insurance excess, and trying to limit the damage to himself and that he had been accepting he had been negligent. Mr Smith denied all of this.

It is worth noting again, the compensation paid to Mr Freeman and Mr Turner was not an insurance excess. The insurance company had not taken control of the claims.

Roger Jones Ltd. was free to accept or reject the claims just as an uninsured company would be able to do. The claims were effectively outside of the insurance, and to be reimbursed by John Smith, Roger Jones Ltd. would have to justify its decisions to settle them. It is common sense that, if you are going to hold someone else responsible for the consequences of your decision, you must be able to justify it.

Miss Brown put to Mr Smith he should have included the defects at Mr Turner's house in his survey report and, particularly, the rotten beam. Mr Smith said he had reported that the conservatory was a condition 3 zone and he had not specifically identified the beam as he had been writing a HomeBuyer Report, which was intended to be brief and concise.

Mr Smith was asked about the woodworm in Mr Freeman's house and recalled there had been a lot of items being stored in the garage by the vendor.

Mr Smith confirmed he had had no involvement with Mr Turner's complaint at the time of the ombudsman's involvement.

Re-examination of John Smith

Mr Smith confirmed at no time had he admitted having been negligent in relation to either of the survey reports.

Note the judge did not ask Mr Smith if it was his evidence that the defects which were the subject of the trial would have been noted regardless of whether it was a Building Survey or a HomeBuyer Report as she had done with Mr Jones. Whilst it might be said how Mr Smith would have answered was obvious, the same might have been said of Mr Jones, yet the judge still asked him the question. It appeared the judge was only interested in the expert opinion of Mr Jones and not that of Mr Smith.

The defendant's closing speech

I represented to the judge that the key issue was whether Mr Smith had been negligent such that the company had had a legal liability to compensate Mr Freeman and Mr Turner.

For the reasons I have already set out, I argued the notion of the insurance excess was irrelevant.

I pointed out that no offer by Mr Smith to pay Mr Turner had led to a binding agreement that Mr Smith should pay anything.

I stated there had been no admission of liability.

Regarding Mr Freeman's property, I said it was difficult to find a breach of duty by Mr Smith because of the time gap between Mr Smith's and Mr Jones's inspections, which meant it was uncertain what woodworm evidence, if any, had been visible to Mr Smith. Further, Mr Jones had accepted Mr Freeman had not overpaid for the property and, therefore, Mr Smith had complied with his duty as set out in the contract for the survey report. As for "loss of chance", I represented there was insufficient evidence before the court to allow the issue to be assessed. I pointed out that Mr Jones had accepted Mr Freeman would have bought the house even if he had known of the woodworm and, therefore, there was no causation.

Regarding the shower in Mr Turner's property, I explained Mr Jones had accepted he could not say it had been dripping when Mr Smith carried out his inspection and, in any event, an expert was not required to see such. Further, the documentary evidence showed Mr Jones had written to Mr Turner telling him a dripping shower would not be included in a HomeBuyer Report.

Regarding the conservatory in Mr Turner's property, I reminded the judge that Mr Smith had identified it as requiring further inspection on a serious and urgent basis and in his written statement he said he had verbally told Mr Turner about the risks to the conservatory and that it would be expensive to repair. I said Mr Jones had vigorously rejected Mr Turner's complaint.

Regarding Mr Turner's calculation of the repair costs, I explained he had ultimately sought £600 for the conservatory and £345 for the shower, yet he had earlier stated the shower repair had actually cost him only £200. I said at best he was entitled to £800 for he was not entitled to the return of his survey fee. Since he had been offered £925 at an early stage, costs which were incurred subsequently had been caused by his unreasonable behaviour.

I pointed out that Mr Jones had accepted Mr Turner had not overpaid for his property. I represented that, in fact, he had underpaid for it since Mr Smith had valued it at £348,000, yet Mr Turner had paid only £340,000 and, clearly, £800 of repairs does not bring about an £8,000 price reduction. Mr Jones, I said, had accepted there had been no diminution in value which, in correspondence, Borders Solicitors had accepted as the appropriate measure of damages. I reminded the judge that Mr Jones had accepted that, had Mr Turner known of the defects, he would still have bought the house so there was no causation, and I referred the judge to an example of that principle being applied by the High Court[6].

Finally, I directed the judge to a House of Lords decision[7] to the effect that, in a case of breach of a duty to take care to provide accurate information (as here), you ask what loss is attributable to the inaccuracy of the information and which the claimant has suffered by reason of (in this case) buying the house on the assumption the information was correct, and you compare the loss suffered with what the purchaser's position would have been if he had not bought the house (it should be

6   K/S Lincoln et al v CB Richard Ellis Hotels Ltd. [2010] All ER (D) 138.

7   South Australia Asset Management Corporation v York Montague Ltd. [1996].

noted the words "attributable" and "by reason of" go directly to the issues of causation and the "but for" principle, so in both Mr Freeman's and Mr Turner's cases, the answer to that question was "none"). I argued this meant that, as long as the purchasers had not overpaid for their properties, they were no worse off than if they had not bought the houses since had they not done so they would still have their money, but having bought them they each had a house of the same or greater value as that money. I referred the judge to two Court of Appeal cases[8] to the effect that the measure of loss in cases of surveyor's negligence is diminution in value and, I argued, the House of Lords case meant the relevant question was simply, "Had the purchaser overpaid?", which was consistent with, and supportive of, the test being diminution in value.

Throughout my attempt to make this closing speech, I had to suffer more icy scowls from the judge and her, by now usual, glances at the wall clock such that it was not possible for me to say everything I wanted to say. Yet I had said enough. It was my view the law and the evidence were overwhelmingly in favour of Mr Smith.

The claimant's closing speech

Miss Brown returned to the three points of her opening address.

She asked the judge to consider whether there was an agreement between the company and Mr Smith that the latter would "be responsible for claims of this nature". She said the parties both accepted Mr Smith was to have paid costs such as the phone, car mileage and insurance premiums. She maintained the evidence showed Mr Smith would pay claims within the insurance excess. Such evidence, she said, included Mr Smith's

---

8   a) Smith & another v Peter North & Partners [2001] All ER (D)
     89 and b) Patel & another v Hooper & Jackson [1998] All ER (D)
     566.

offer to pay Mr Turner. She pointed out that Mr Jones had said in his statement that Mr Smith had made a second offer to pay Mr Turner in the sum of £2,500. She questioned why Mr Smith would make such offers simply as a matter of goodwill if he believed the company would pay any insurance excess and the insurers would pay any amount over the excess.

She said her second point had been to ask whether Mr Smith had been negligent, and she confirmed this was a different and alternative argument to point one. She pointed to the fact that the ombudsman had found a payment should be made to Mr Turner, and, she said, there was the view of Mr Jones, an expert, that on all the information available to him it had been right to make the payments.

Her third point, she said, had been quantum (i.e. how much had the company been liable to pay each client), and, although the judge had before her case decisions of the higher courts to the effect that quantum should be based on valuation (i.e. diminution in value), she argued this case was different as it involved very small sums of money such as justified the judge departing from the higher court decisions (which, otherwise, she was bound to follow).

I have commented earlier in this chapter that the idea that, pursuant to some agreement by Mr Smith to pay the costs of his engagement by the company, he should pay for damages to complainants (whether or not they were legally entitled to anything) is wrong.

Miss Brown was here saying Mr Smith was liable for the excess on the insurance (denied by Mr Smith), but she was overlooking the fact that this was not a case where the amount exceeded the insurance excess such that the insurers had taken control and made the decisions whether the company liked them or not. That fact meant the insurance was irrelevant, and the fact the amount paid out by the company was less than the value of the insurance excess (in the same way it is true to say two is less than four) did not make it relevant. Again, I say, the company had a choice to settle or dispute the claims, and it had to justify why it chose to settle.

Miss Brown referred to Mr Smith's offer to pay Mr Turner £2,500, an offer Mr Jones refused to sanction. This offer was clearly not, on any view, a sensible offer which reflected the cost of repairs facing Mr Turner (hence Roger Jones's refusal to sanction it). Miss Brown was saying the offer meant Mr Smith saw himself as responsible to pay compensation, but could it not just as easily be said such an irrational offer indicated Mr Smith just wanted the matter out of the way, as he had said in his evidence?

When in her opening speech Miss Brown had asked had it been right to make the payments, she had made it clear she meant had the company acted to keep the loss to a minimum and made a "sensible commercial decision", and she can be taken to mean that here and not to be referring to whether the company had been right to pay out pursuant to a true legal liability.

Although she was accepting her first and second points were alternative arguments, she did not present her third point as alternative to points one and two, and she did not explain its relevance. Diminution in value arose as an issue only if the company had been legally liable to compensate the clients, and Miss Brown had not explained how that issue fitted in with her arguments about an agreement to pay costs and the company having been right to make the payments. What was she saying its relevance was? She was clearly accepting there had been no diminution in value to the clients' properties because she was arguing that the cost of repairs was the right legal test. She wanted the judge to make that ruling, in support of an argument the clients had been owed compensation by the company (an argument which rejects the "but for" principle), but why did that matter if the company was entitled to recover from Mr Smith on the basis of an agreement to pay costs or because it had acted reasonably? It was not clear. It was clear she considered the issue of "what had the company been legally obliged to pay to the clients?" to be relevant (and of some importance given one of her three points turned on that question).

Her notion that this case should not have the diminution in value principle applied to it because the cost of the repairs was low is not obviously logical. If the test is diminution in value, it would seem strange not to apply it in circumstances where there was least likely to be diminution in value. It was as if she was saying that because the correct legal test meant the purchasers were not entitled to anything, would the court please apply the wrong test as it helped her client's case! The judge was legally bound to follow the rulings of the higher courts unless there was good reason to see this case as being materially different; there was no case decision provided by Miss Brown to support her argument, and it did not appear rational. In one of the higher court decisions[9] I had presented to the judge, the Court of Appeal had decided the prima facie rule applicable to the measure of damages in respect of negligent surveys of houses is the diminution in value of the property.

Although the defendant at a trial does not give a reply to the final speech of the claimant, both parties should participate in any point of law that is raised, yet the judge did not invite my views on Miss Brown's assertion that diminution in value did not apply because of the low value of the cost of repairs.

Other arguments such as those relating to the ombudsman's fee, the return of the survey fee to Mr Turner and, crucially, the "but for" principle were equally valid as that of diminution in value but, notably, were not commented on by Miss Brown.

Miss Brown in her closing speech did not rely on the "loss of chance" argument, one of my pre-trial concerns. My other two concerns, namely, had the insurers taken control and, in

---

9   Patel & another v Hooper & Jackson [1998] All ER (D) 566.

Mr Turner's case alone, had an offer to pay by Mr Smith created a binding agreement, had been resolved by the evidence in Mr Smith's favour. The judgment should be a slam dunk.

The judgment

The judge found Mr Jones to have been an honest and fair witness and his recollection of the facts to have been accurate. She found he had entered into negotiations with disgruntled clients, as he was obliged to do.

In Mr Turner's case, she found the decision to instruct and utilise the ombudsman to have been fair and valid. She found the ombudsman's decision to have been well founded, and this, she said, together with Mr Smith having offered to pay £925 to Mr Turner, meant the decision by Mr Jones to settle the matter out of court had been proportionate and valid based on the information he had at that time. She found Mr Smith's offer to pay Mr Turner was an admission of his culpability, warranting the payment of monies. She found Mr Smith should have included in his report the defects at Mr Turner's house, and she accepted Mr Jones's evidence that the defects would have been clear and could easily have been in the report.

In Mr Freeman's case, she found it was not clear the woodworm would have been evident at the time of Mr Smith's inspection.

Regarding the law, she accepted Miss Brown's argument that this case was different to the higher courts' decisions since it involved smaller sums of money (i.e. she found the correct measure of damages to Mr Turner was the cost of the repairs and not diminution in value).

Returning to Mr Turner's case, she repeated that Mr Jones had been obliged to settle the matter, and, she said, he had done so in court proceedings pursuant to the overriding objective of proportionality, and the settlement had been proportional.

She found insufficient information to support the claim for £100 administration costs, which she disallowed.

She found the payment of the ombudsman's fee to have been "necessitous".

She made no mention of "loss of chance".

Accordingly, she dismissed the claim relating to Mr Freeman's house, and in respect of Mr Turner's claim, she awarded the company the £1,250 (being the settlement paid to Mr Turner) and the £260 ombudsman's fee.

During her judgment, the judge had said, "I look towards the law" and "I have looked at the provisions of the law within this case". Really? She should have turned around. In my opinion, and metaphorically speaking, the judge was simply protesting her innocence whilst committing the crime.

She dismissed the claim relating to Mr Freeman, but let us look closer at her decision regarding Mr Turner's complaint.

She did not make clear whether she found Mr Smith to be at fault in relation to both the conservatory and the shower.

She did not deal with the "but for" principle or with Mr Turner's lack of entitlement to the return of his survey fee.

In fact, she did not deal fully with why the company owed a legal liability to Mr Turner and what that liability was. It is clear her judgment found such a liability, and, therefore, she thought it relevant, otherwise, there would have been no need to rule on the measure of damages being the cost of repairs and not diminution in value. She jumped from Mr Smith having been negligent (presumably regarding both the conservatory and the shower – who knows?!) to the measure of damages being the cost of repairs, thereby missing out altogether the issue of causation.

She found Mr Jones to have been an honest and fair witness, yet this was the man who had claimed damages were an agreed cost, lied to Mr Turner in a letter denying liability and initially said Mr Turner was "pretty sharp" but quickly changed that to "determined"!

Generally, the judge seemed to have followed Miss Brown's three-point approach though she did not expressly say she had applied the fact there had been an agreement to pay costs associated with Mr Smith's engagement.

She found Mr Jones had been obliged to enter into negotiations with a disgruntled client, but that did not tell us that Mr Turner had suffered a legally recoverable loss or that he had behaved reasonably. It was necessary to consider what had really caused the company a problem. Early in the negotiations, Mr Turner was offered £925, which Mr Smith had been willing to pay even though there had been no legal liability to pay anything. Mr Smith would have been entitled to say he would pay nothing. That would have been a reasonable, responsible and legally correct decision, yet he had gone far beyond that with the offer of £925. When Mr Turner unreasonably or mistakenly rejected that offer, why was Mr Smith liable for what ensued? Even if Mr Smith had made a mistake with his survey report, by offering to pay £925 he had acted more than responsibly to put matters right at an early stage, offering more than Mr Turner would ultimately accept for the cost of repairs. What more could he have done? In fact, he later offered £2,500, but Mr Jones would not sanction that so Jones himself was in part the author of what followed thereafter. It would be tempting to say none of what happened would have happened if indeed Mr Smith had not made a mistake with his report, but that does not look at the real cause of what occurred. If a husband is nasty to his wife one morning and, angry, she leaves in the car and is killed when a drunk driver ploughs into her, would you say her husband killed her because she would not have got into her car if he had not been nasty to her? Consider that a client complained about Mr Smith in circumstances in which there was no suggestion Mr Smith had been at fault. The client would be owed nothing, but his complaint might cost the company time and trouble, yet by his own evidence Mr Jones would not have sought recompense from Mr Smith (he had said he would not be asking for reimbursement from Mr Smith if he had not been negligent). Compare that to a situation in which Mr Smith had been at fault, but the client had lost nothing and was owed nothing, yet he pursued a complaint. The two scenarios have in common the fact that the client was owed nothing. Why in one instance, and not the other, should Mr Smith be responsible for the cost and time of the client's mistaken complaint? Now throw into the equation the fact that Mr Smith had offered at an early stage to pay £925 and later Mr Jones blocked the offer by Mr Smith to pay the silly amount of £2,500 – whose fault was it that Mr Turner's complaint continued?

She found the decision to instruct the ombudsman to have been fair and valid. How could that be so when he achieved nothing more than the company had already offered him and, mostly, he was complaining about fire damage, a complaint he would later abandon? If his complaint had been fair and valid, that would only have signified that the company had failed to deal with his complaint properly in the first place, which was clearly not the case.

She found the ombudsman's decision to have been well founded, yet it included the reimbursement of the survey fee, which Mr Turner was not legally entitled to (an issue the judge did not comment on). Further, the judge should have found the ombudsman's decision that £500 should be paid for the conservatory did not reflect any legal liability since the "but for" principle (another issue the judge did not deal with) alone meant Mr Turner was entitled to nothing. As a reflection of the true legal liability, the ombudsman's decision was wholly unfounded. The judge also, seemingly, ignored the fact that the ombudsman made no award for the dripping shower, a complaint which he had clearly rejected.

Although she did not say so, it seemed to me possible the judge was treating the ombudsman's fee as a cost associated with

Mr Smith's engagement. Even Mr Jones had not said Mr Smith had agreed at the outset he would pay an ombudsman's fee as a cost, and such would not generally be considered a cost which would occur in the normal course of working for a company. If the company had wanted this sort of thing to be treated as a cost, there surely should have been a detailed written contract. Also, had this fee been incurred because of Mr Smith's engagement, or had it been caused by an unreasonable or mistaken complaint by Mr Turner? Further, a cost would not generally depend on Mr Smith having made a mistake, yet the company would not have looked to him to pay this fee if he had not made an error (so Mr Jones had said in his evidence). Treating the ombudsman's fee as a cost associated with Mr Smith's engagement (if that is what the judge did) made no sense and ran contrary to the evidence.

She found Mr Smith's offer to pay to be an admission of liability. Well, no specific offer had been made regarding the dripping shower so how had he admitted liability for that? Also, regarding the conservatory, there was plenty of evidence Mr Smith had complied with his duty. Even if the judge was entitled to find Mr Smith had admitted he should have mentioned the conservatory defects in the report, that admission would not encompass the issues of causation and loss.

She found Mr Jones's decision to settle with Mr Turner had, on the information available to him, been proportionate and valid and pursuant to an obligation on parties involved in court proceedings to act proportionately. This latter point is one I mentioned in the Pre-trial chapter; namely, that cases should be dealt with "justly and at proportionate cost". The judge actually referred to "the overriding objective of proportionality", thereby omitting the word "justly"! Amongst other things, "justly" means a party is not obliged to pay compensation where there is no legal liability to do so, and the company had clearly owed Mr Turner nothing. A person is entitled to dispute a claim in full (when you file your written defence, the form asks if that is what you want to do), and "proportionately" simply refers to the appropriate procedure by which the court and the parties deal with the dispute. Had the company fought Mr Turner's hopeless and unfounded court claim to the bitter end that would not have fallen foul of any obligation to act proportionately. As to the information available to Mr Jones, he had had all the relevant information he needed to be able to reject Mr Turner's complaint. He had lacked nothing. I wondered if, in referring to the information available, the judge was alluding to the solicitors' advice given to the company, but no competent judge would think that relevant so that idea could be dismissed out of hand. What the judge really seemed to be saying was that Mr Jones had dealt with Mr Turner in a commercially sensible way, but this was not a trial in the local Chamber of Commerce! If the legal test in a case such as this was, "The contractor having breached his duty of care, did the company thereafter act proportionately or reasonably?", contractors such as Mr Smith would be on a hiding to nothing and companies would make little effort to fight complaints brought by clients, for all they would need to do is be seen not to have acted unreasonably in dealing with the complaint – the dice would be stacked very much in companies' favour. Also, what would happen in a case where a client complains about several mistakes by the surveyor, and his complaint is only valid for some but not all of those mistakes, yet the company, even though the client has in part suffered no loss for which the company is legally liable, compensates him for all of them and unnecessarily pays back his survey fee? Was that not the case here if a mistake had been made regarding the conservatory but not the shower? Why didn't the company throw in Christmas presents for Mr Turner, his wife and his children also?! Was Mr Smith responsible for Mr Turner's vexatious, apparently fraudulent, unreasonable and mistaken complaint? Was Mr Smith responsible for the ombudsman's lack of legal knowledge and his mistaken decision (this assumes the ombudsman was making a decision intended to reflect the true legal liability and not simply choosing to leave the company's goodwill offer on the table)? Was Mr Smith responsible for the legal advice given to the company? Was Mr Smith responsible for the company's legally flawed decision not to go to trial with Mr Turner but, rather, to pay him when he had been owed nothing?

The judge accepted Miss Brown's argument that because this case involved small sums of money the diminution in value test was not appropriate. Like Miss Brown, she did not explain why she thought this distinction relevant and rational, yet she clearly did. She had found relevant the issue of what legal liability the company had owed to Mr Turner – why then did she not deal with the "but for" principle and the issue of the survey fee? In deciding the cost of repairs, and not diminution in value, was the appropriate measure of damages, the judge had also implicitly found against the "but for" principle since the issue as to cost of repairs or diminution in value does not arise if the claim fails on the "but for" test – you have to get past the "but for" test before you need to ask what the measure of damages is! In finding the cost of repairs to be appropriate, she had, seemingly, acted contrary to case decisions of the higher courts, which were legally binding upon her unless this case was materially different, yet she did not explain why low-value repair costs were a material difference and no case authority was identified in support of her decision. That the cost of repairs is low and does not result in a diminution in value of the property, is surely the whole point of the diminution in value test: damages arise only if the repairs are so serious the value of your house has gone down. The judge's rationale appears to be that the further away the cost of repairs is from affecting the value of the property, the more likely it is to be allowed, which seems to be the contrary intention to the diminution in value test. It was incumbent upon her to explain why low-value repair costs meant diminution in value was not the test.

Costs and fees

A discussion ensued between the judge and Miss Brown as to the costs and fees to which the company was entitled, with the judge helping counsel not to miss anything out. There was the initial court fee of £115, a trial fee of £170, travel expenses of £72, witness expenses for Mr Jones of £90 (loss of earnings for his morning at court) and interest of £69.83. There then arose two matters which would become of great importance later.

Firstly, Miss Brown claimed the £80 legal representative's costs mentioned on the claim form. I represented to the judge that those costs were not allowable when there had been a trial. The judge said, "Well, unless you have that regulation with you, that's not my understanding", and Miss Brown mockingly joked, "That's something I'll be very interested in. I'll be using that a lot." Amongst my papers, I could not readily find the relevant regulation (though the judge had the regulations beside her), and so the judge allowed the £80.

Secondly, Mr Jones was paying Miss Brown a fee of £300 for her conduct of the trial. I mentioned earlier[10] that the general rule for small claims is a successful party cannot recover legal fees from the losing party. I also mentioned that an exception to that rule is where the losing party has behaved unreasonably in its conduct of the case. It followed, the only way the company could recover its payment of Miss Brown's £300 fee was to allege I had conducted the case unreasonably. Miss Brown argued it had been unreasonable that Mr Smith had not participated in the mediation service offered by the court, that my correspondence had been beyond what was normally acceptable for a small claim and that some of it had been sent at very unsociable hours. The correspondence, she said, had led Mr Jones to incur extensive legal fees. Let us look more closely at all this.

---

10   See the Demand chapter.

The courts like parties to use the mediation service as it is an attempt to get them to agree on a settlement and avoid an unnecessary trial. Yet what is the point of mediation if you have no intention of settling and you believe your arguments are correct? To mediate in such circumstances is just to waste everyone's time. Further, Borders Solicitors and I were corresponding, and we were more than capable of reaching any agreement had one been possible.

Unnecessary correspondence should not be sent whether the case is a small claim or not. There is an obligation on the parties to try to reduce the case issues to the bare minimum for the trial, i.e. the parties should try to agree as much as possible. That is done through correspondence. There is also an obligation on a party to draw the court's attention to any relevant law and to send any case reports relied on to the other party.

Miss Brown complained of correspondence at unsocial hours. This was emails sent in the middle of the night when I found myself working on the case. Surely these were picked up the following morning and caused no disturbance to the receiver? If a mobile phone was sounding each time an email was received, the settings could have been changed accordingly. Further, what had this to do with Miss Brown's £300 trial fee – would her fee have been less if the emails had been sent at sociable hours?!

Miss Brown referred to "extensive legal fees", yet she was only asking the judge for her fee of £300 for that day. Why was she not asking the judge for the extensive fees to which she had referred, and why did she refer to them if she was not asking for them? It did not make any sense. I do not believe there were any such fees. You will remember I said earlier[11] that a company is not likely to incur thousands of pounds of legal fees in order to recover £2,000, yet Borders Solicitors had been involved. That made no sense. I believe Mr Jones knew someone at Borders

---

11   See the Demand chapter.

who was prepared to conduct the case free of charge as a favour. Consistent with that view is the fact that, after filing the written defence, Borders officially withdrew from the case leaving Mr Jones on his own. Shortly afterwards, when my correspondence became too much for Mr Jones, Borders started to deal once more, but they did not make that official on the court record. When it came to the trial, Mr Jones had clearly thought it worthwhile to pay Miss Brown £300 to act, but I believe that was the full extent of his legal fees.

The judge denied Miss Brown's application, pointing out that the defence had been concise, valid and, in part, had succeeded.

The judge awarded a grand total of £2,106.83.

The judge

I have strongly criticised the judge, but do you think that fair? After all, she dismissed the claim so far as it related to Mr Freeman's house, she did not award the £100 administration costs and she refused the application for Miss Brown's £300 fee. On the other hand, it might be said a biased person is not necessarily stupid and, by throwing a couple of small fish to Mr Smith, the judge sought to disguise her wrongdoing. It might also be said that the application for the £300 was just asking too much even of a biased judge.

Instead of trying to prove anything against this judge, it is perhaps more helpful if I set out my experience of her: I felt towards me she was unpleasant, rude and disrespectful; she was biased; she was more concerned with time than the evidence and the law; and she sought to intimidate and neutralise me – she was a bully. Looking at her conduct as a whole and the quality of her judgment, do you think she acted with bias and deliberately ignored the law?

A recap

It is easy for the essence to be lost amidst the myriad facts and arguments so, in summary, I will try to give my opinion in a nutshell.

The judge was entitled to find Mr Smith should have included the rotten timber in the conservatory in his report, even though I considered she was wrong to do so. She was not entitled to find he should have mentioned the shower.

The judge found the company had had a legal liability to compensate Mr Turner. We know this because she decided the cost of repairs and not diminution in value was the appropriate measure of damages, an issue that would not have arisen if the "but for" principle applied. That meant she had found against the application of that principle. On the evidence, it was unarguable that the "but for" principle meant Mr Turner had been owed nothing – common sense and the evidence, which included an admission by Mr Jones to the effect the "but for" rule applied in Mr Smith's favour, said so. The argument was in the written defence, the evidence and in my final speech, and in her judgment the judge made clear she was aware of it (although she did not deal with it, she referred to it when summarising the defence arguments). It is impossible to believe the judge simply overlooked it. It was clear and beyond doubt. Why did she not apply it?

Prima facie, the correct measure of damages in a case of surveyor's negligence is diminution in value.

Mr Turner was not entitled to the return of his survey fee.

Mr Turner's complaint was mistaken and unreasonable, and it had led to the costs incurred by the company, including the ombudsman's fee and the court fee.

There was no evidence that the ombudsman's fee had been agreed as a cost of Mr Smith's engagement.

The rule that cases should be conducted "justly and proportionately" has no application to one party's liability to another such that the company had been "obliged" to settle Mr Turner's court claim.

The idea that the legal test in establishing Mr Smith's liability to Roger Jones Ltd. was whether the company had handled the complaint reasonably or proportionately is wholly misconceived.

The insurance excess was irrelevant. The company had been free to decide how to deal with Mr Turner's claim, and it had to justify the decision it had taken.

THE APPEAL

"Law without justice is a wound without a cure."

William Scott Downey, *Proverbs*

With whatever motive, in so far as the case related to Mr Turner, the district judge had got matters badly wrong. The notion that if Mr Smith had made a mistake, all the company had to do thereafter was to act reasonably and proportionately was, in my view, plainly wrong and was certainly a legitimate point of appeal. The evidence that Mr Smith had made a mistake was manifestly inadequate regarding the supposedly dripping shower and, in my view, in Mr Smith's favour regarding the rotten conservatory timber. There was no evidence Mr Smith had agreed to pay as a cost of his engagement any ombudsman's fee or payment directed by the ombudsman. Even if Mr Smith had been negligent, the "but for" principle, without any shadow of a doubt, meant Mr Turner had not been entitled to anything from the company. If all that was not enough, there were the points relating to the survey fee, diminution in value, the legal representative's costs and more besides. An appeal looked a racing certainty in favour of Mr Smith, and he decided to appeal.

An appeal from a small claim trial is to a circuit judge of the County Court. A circuit judge is a middle-ranking judge in the judicial hierarchy. When you file an appeal, you set out in writing your arguments as to why the district judge's decision was wrong, or unjust because of a serious procedural or other irregularity, and you pay a fee, which was £120 in Mr Smith's case. The appeal is a two-stage process. You ask for permission to appeal, and, if that is granted, the appeal will be heard in open court. In deciding whether to grant permission, the judge will consider your written arguments and any accompanying documents, and if the appeal has a real prospect of success, permission will be granted. If the circuit judge refuses permission to appeal, normally, you will be given the option of attending court to try in person to persuade a judge to grant permission. The cost of the appeal is irrelevant, so a judge cannot refuse permission because the case is too trivial to justify the time and money involved in dealing with it.

I drafted the appeal, and, suffice it to say, I provided the appeal judge with all the relevant facts, evidence, arguments and law references (including copy case decisions from the higher courts). I did not argue that, due to bias or lack of time, the trial had been procedurally unjust since, with appeal courts bending over backwards to avoid such a finding, such arguments rarely succeed. I argued only that the judge had been wrong, albeit on many points. Roger Jones Ltd. did not participate at this stage, and so the application for permission simply had to succeed without opposition from the company. Remember, at this stage, the judge was not being asked to decide the appeal but, rather, was being asked to accept it merited a hearing at which the arguments could be fully considered.

Dated 23rd March 2015, this was the circuit judge's ruling:

"The application is dismissed for the following reasons:

The Defendant has no real prospect of success.

REASONS: – On the evidence, the District Judge was entitled to find that the Defendant breached his duty of care and that the breach caused the Claimants to suffer the loss claimed. The Defendant concedes that the District Judge found his evidence "implausible" and that there were defects which he failed to mention in his report. The District Judge was entitled to prefer the written evidence. Pursuant to CPR r 27.14, the District Judge may order one party to pay the Court fees, expenses, and further costs if that party has behaved unreasonably.

The above ruling having been made without an oral hearing, the Defendant may within 7 days of receipt of this order request such a hearing before His [sic] Honour Judge (name). If the Defendant requests an oral hearing it shall be listed for 30 minutes and the Defendant shall obtain and file a transcript of the Judgement [sic] of District Judge (name) in advice [sic] of the hearing."

When I first read this ruling, I immediately believed the appeal had been dismissed for illegitimate reasons. Notwithstanding the promise of the *Magna Carta* that no one would be denied right or justice; notwithstanding the rule of law's core concept "… that all persons and authorities within the state, whether public or private, should be bound by and entitled to the benefit of laws publicly and prospectively promulgated and publicly administered in the courts" (see Lord Bingham's *Eight Principles of the Rule of Law*) and its promise that "Ministers and public officers at all levels must exercise the powers conferred on them reasonably, in good faith, for the purpose for which the powers were conferred and without exceeding the limit of such powers" (Bingham's sixth principle); and notwithstanding the judge's oath of office to "do right to all manner of people after the laws and usages of this realm, without fear or favour, affection or ill will"; I believed the appeal had been blocked despite its obvious merits. I believed a judge, charged with the solemn duty of applying the law and delivering justice, had deliberately acted to defeat justice. The right to a fair appeal is given to us by Parliament, not by judges, and I believed a judge had thwarted Parliament, the elected chamber which is our chief lawmaker and whose will is sovereign. Worse still, Mr Smith had paid a fee of £120 for the privilege, a fee he was not going to get back.

My belief amounted to a very serious accusation against the circuit judge. Let's have a closer look at her ruling.

"The Defendant has no real prospect of success"

With this the judge dismisses the appeal and all its arguments. It is the legal test set out by the rules, and any refusal to grant permission will include this statement. It says that my arguments are hopeless.

"On the evidence, the District Judge was entitled to find that the Defendant breached his duty of care..."

As I have said, it is arguable the district judge was wrong to find Mr Smith should have mentioned the rotten timber in the conservatory. Here, the circuit judge finds this not to be arguable. My accusation against her does not depend upon that ruling.

But what about the supposedly dripping shower? There are two alleged breaches of duty, one regarding the defects in the conservatory and the other regarding the dripping shower, yet the circuit judge does not deal with them separately. The evidence the shower had been dripping at the time of the survey by Mr Smith had been the word of Mr Turner, who did not attend court in person and who had given contradictory figures for the cost of the repairs. Mr Smith had made no offer of payment specifically for the shower and cannot thereby be taken to have admitted negligence regarding it. Further, the ombudsman had not directed any payment for the shower. It is very hard to understand why the circuit judge, seemingly, upholds a breach of duty in relation to the shower.

My doubts as to her motives began.

"On the evidence, the District Judge was entitled to find... that the breach caused the Claimants to suffer the loss claimed."

This is very vague. It just says, "you're wrong". In the appeal, I had highlighted the "but for" principle and its application to the case; I had complained Mr Turner had not been entitled to the return of his survey fee; I had dealt in detail with the diminution in value principle and enclosed copies of the cases of the higher courts; I had made clear all the facts which showed Mr Turner had been offered £925 at an early stage, that his complaint to the ombudsman and his subsequent court action had been misconceived and that the evidence regarding the shower was inadequate; I had set out why the "reasonable and proportionate behaviour" test was not the correct legal test; and I had even mentioned those arguments, such as "loss of chance", that might have worked against Mr Smith but had come to nothing at the trial. I had covered everything, yet the judge here pours scorn on it all, declaring none of it to have even any prospect of success. It beggars belief – the arguments in favour of Mr Smith are entirely in accordance with basic legal principles and with legal precedent which is binding on this judge. What is she doing?

In my opinion, particularly on the issues of causation and loss, it is inconceivable a judge, honestly performing her duty, could rule the arguments put forward in the appeal have no real prospect of success; the evidence, the law and common sense are all overwhelmingly in favour of Mr Smith's position. The trial judge wrongly found the "but for" principle did not apply, and that affected the validity of her entire judgment. Every aspect of her findings on causation and loss unquestionably justified granting permission to appeal. Why then is the circuit judge not allowing this appeal to move forward? It is inexplicable. My doubts as to this judge's motives deepened.

"The Defendant concedes that the District Judge found his evidence implausible…"

This finding of the trial judge was conceded in the appeal I drafted. At trial, Mr Smith had maintained his offer to pay compensation to Mr Turner had not been because he thought he had been negligent. The trial judge had disagreed, finding his evidence implausible. This finding of the circuit judge simply relates to the ruling she has already made, namely, that the trial judge had been entitled to find Mr Smith had breached his duty of care. Really, it adds nothing to the circuit judge's decision, but it operates to make Mr Smith look bad.

"The Defendant concedes… that there were defects which he failed to mention in his report."

The appeal made no such concession, and this is a curious inclusion for at no stage had Mr Smith denied the specific defects complained of by Mr Turner had not been included in the report. However, Mr Smith had never conceded he had "failed" to include them. Firstly, he had maintained there had been no defect to the shower, and you cannot fail to include a defect which does not exist. Secondly, he had maintained the defects to the conservatory had been adequately dealt with, by what he had said in his report and in person to Mr Turner, such that it had not been necessary to mention the specifics later complained of. So, the circuit judge is wrong to use the word "failed" when referring to any concession made by or on behalf of Mr Smith. This error by the circuit judge also operates to make Mr Smith look bad. Amongst other things, her judgment appears to be unbalanced to Mr Smith's prejudice.

"The District Judge was entitled to prefer the written evidence."

There are two things wrong with this statement. Firstly, the circuit judge does not mention what evidence she has in mind, without which it is meaningless. Secondly, there was no written evidence at the trial that supported the claimant's case. Oh, there was the survey report which showed the specific defects complained of were not present, but that was not disputed and, actually, the report helped Mr Smith as he had given the conservatory zone a category 3 condition rating, which was the equivalent of sticking a flashing red light on it; there was a document showing the ombudsman had left in place the goodwill offer of £925, but it did not show the reasons for doing so, and it did not include anything for the shower; there was the front page of Mr Turner's claim form from his suit against the company, which showed he was claiming the refund of his survey fee and more for the shower than he had previously said it had cost. This was all very helpful to Mr Smith but not to Mr Turner. So, to what evidence is she referring?

This general, meaningless statement by the circuit judge sounds judicial and considered, but, without identifying the documents and their relevance, it does not stand up to scrutiny, and it arouses suspicion that there is no substance behind it and it is masking what is really going on.

"Pursuant to CPR r 27.14, the District Judge may order one party to pay the Court fees, expenses, and further costs if that party has behaved unreasonably."

If you have not yet been persuaded to have serious concerns about the circuit judge's decision, this finding might resolve any doubt you may have. It offends against common sense, the relevant legal rules and natural justice. It is a disgrace.

"CPR r 27.14" refers to Rule 14 of Part 27 of the Civil Procedure Rules 1998. The judge's statement is not a direct quote from the rule and, in fact, the rule deals in three distinct and different sub-paragraphs with court fees, expenses and "further costs where a party has behaved unreasonably". The rule also deals with other types of costs that may be ordered such as experts' fees, loss of earnings and fixed costs attributable to issuing the claim, but these are not mentioned by the circuit judge, so she should have a reason for mentioning the three she sets out. You will remember that the trial judge ordered Mr Smith should pay the £80 legal representative costs included on the claim form and that these were fixed costs attributable to issuing the claim. In the appeal, I complained that the trial judge had been wrong to make that order and, although she does not expressly say so, the circuit judge is dealing here with that aspect of the appeal. I have the following comments:

1. The circuit judge clearly accepts the trial judge got it wrong. She does not say the trial judge was right to order the £80 as fixed costs. The rules are crystal clear, she has no direct answer and, acting without fear or favour, she should not be looking for one. So why does she not allow the appeal to go ahead on this point? It should be that simple – the trial judge erred, the appeal looks good and so it goes ahead. What is motivating her not to act in that way?

2. Why does the circuit judge mention court fees and expenses? As I have said, the rule deals in three distinct and different sub-paragraphs with these two types of costs and the "further costs where a party has behaved unreasonably", so they do not naturally come together in a direct quote from the rule. Why then does the judge draw them together in her decision? The trial judge ordered Mr Smith should pay court fees and expenses and there was no appeal against that (such would automatically be extinguished if other grounds of appeal succeeded). Court fees and expenses do not cover legal representative's costs, and they are wholly irrelevant to the appeal. So why does the circuit judge mention them? If a judge includes something in a judgment, there must be a reason for it. Are they meant to make the order appear more judicial and considered in order to mask its lack of substance? The mention of court fees and expenses is inexplicable.

3. The circuit judge's wording here is very strange indeed for it makes no order whatsoever. It simply says the trial judge "**may** order…", but who cares what the trial judge **may** do? What is being appealed is what the trial judge **did** do. The wording used by the circuit judge is meaningless in the context of the appeal, and it is proper once again to ask what on earth is going on. To make any sense of this, we have to help the judge out, which should never be necessary and is, to say the least, highly unsatisfactory. A circuit judge dealing with an appeal has power to do anything the trial judge could have done, and in order to give any sense to her wording we have to interpret her order in that way. So, we have to interpret the wording as meaning the circuit judge is now replacing the trial

judge's mistaken fixed costs order with one which says Mr Smith is ordered to pay the £80 as "court fees, expenses and further costs if that party has behaved unreasonably". But these are three different types of costs, so which one is the judge ordering? The £80 was for legal representative's costs so it can only be covered by the "further costs where a party has behaved unreasonably". By a process of deduction, and in order to give any meaning to this part of the judge's order, we have to conclude the circuit judge is making an order against Mr Smith that the £80 legal representative's costs on the claim form be paid by him because of unreasonable behaviour, and my subsequent comments are based on that conclusion without which no sensible analysis could possibly be made on this point. No other interpretation is possible. The use of the word "may" is so bizarre that, alone, it is reason enough to doubt the motives of this judge.

4. You will recall at trial Miss Brown applied for her £300 fee on the basis that Mr Smith's case had been conducted unreasonably, but the trial judge rejected that request. In the appeal, I made no mention of this. So, what has led the circuit judge to even think of an order for costs due to unreasonable behaviour? It is not a usual order, so what has placed the notion in her mind? She might have scoured through the court file (but why would she?) and seen that an application had been made by Miss Brown (this assumes the trial judge included it in her notes and the circuit judge had reason to read them), but that application was not for the £80 costs on the claim form, and the circuit judge would also have seen that the trial judge had refused the request – all the more reason to reject the notion out of hand. As you will

see later, the fact that the circuit judge even thinks to mention costs based on unreasonable behaviour in her order will, ultimately, provoke Mr Smith to complain to the High Court.

5. Roger Jones Ltd. had made no application based on unreasonable behaviour for the £80 costs! Judges do not make such orders off the cuff and uninvited, and they certainly should not make them to bail out a trial judge who has erred.

6. The £80 costs ordered were for the work of preparing the claim form, so any relevant unreasonable behaviour would have to have occurred before that work was done, otherwise, it could not possibly have caused the costs. Such costs are caused by a defendant rejecting or ignoring the claimant's demands such that the latter decides to sue. If in this regard the defendant knows he has no defence, but simply wants to test the claimant's resolve to see if he will actually sue, that is what the fixed costs provision is there to deal with, and, where the fixed costs do not apply (as here), it is for good reason. It is very difficult to imagine costs based on unreasonable behaviour ever being ordered in relation to pre-claim conduct and certainly not for the work involved in preparing a claim form.

7. There is no evidence on the court file, or otherwise, which comes close to justifying a finding that there had been unreasonable behaviour which caused the unnecessary preparation of the claim form. So, what unreasonable behaviour does the circuit judge have in mind? Yet again, she does not explain herself.

8. How could it be said Mr Smith had unreasonably caused the preparation of the claim form when he had filed a perfectly legitimate written defence (a view expressed by the trial judge), had contested the claim

to trial (and even to appeal) and had partly succeeded at trial?

9. An order for costs based on unreasonable behaviour would not be based on the fixed costs provisions. The former would calculate costs based on a fair hourly rate for the solicitor's work and would not limit itself to £80 – such a calculation would far exceed £80. It is an extraordinary coincidence that the circuit judge's calculation of costs due to unreasonable behaviour happens to come to £80, the exact figure which the trial judge had erroneously ordered! Does that look like a fudge to you?

10. What information does the circuit judge have in order to make her calculation of the costs? There has been no application for these costs by the claimant, so how is she working it out? What hourly rate is she using and why, and how much time had the solicitor spent preparing the claim form? She does not know. She must be guessing.

11. Unlike the circuit judge, the trial judge had heard evidence at the trial, had witnessed the parties conduct and had heard argument from them on the issue of unreasonable behaviour. The trial judge was well placed to make a decision on the point, whereas the circuit judge is not placed to do so at all. Even though Miss Brown's application for £300 had related to trial costs and not the £80 costs of preparing the claim form, it is impossible to conceive of an application for the latter succeeding where the former has failed. After all, if you have unreasonably caused someone to prepare a claim form, how can you not have unreasonably caused the subsequent trial? If I set fire to the hall mat, and the house burns down, my responsibility does not end at the hall mat! By ordering the £80 costs because of

unreasonable behaviour, effectively, the circuit judge is overruling the trial judge's order regarding the £300, yet she does not order the £300! It makes no sense – she's ordering payment for the hall mat but not the house!

12. The most damning criticism of the circuit judge's decision to order costs based on unreasonable behaviour is that she has not told Mr Smith she was thinking of doing so, and why, and she has not given him an opportunity to make representations against it. Nor does her order specify why she is making the ruling or what information she is relying upon. In other words, she is not adopting a fair procedure. Imagine that at work your boss fined you but did not tell you he was thinking of doing so, gave you no opportunity to comment and, subsequently, did not tell you why he had done so. Would you think that fair? Do you think an employment tribunal would say that was a fair procedure? Is this the procedure that one of Her Majesty's judges, acting honestly and in good faith, would adopt? Of course, the judge goes on to offer Mr Smith an oral hearing, but that is closing the stable door after the horse has bolted, and she still is not providing him with her reasons for her decision. Also, as you will see shortly, she places an impediment in the way of his taking advantage of that oral hearing. To this day, despite requests, complaints and a subsequent High Court action, we still do not know why this order was made. It is an absolute disgrace. Why is this judge still in office?

More than any other part of her order, the circuit judge's dismissal of the argument regarding the fixed costs evidences a determination on her part that this appeal should not be allowed to move forward. The mystery is why.

"The above ruling having been made without an oral hearing, the Defendant may within 7 days of receipt of this order request such a hearing before His [sic] Honour Judge (name). If the Defendant requests an oral hearing it shall be listed for 30 minutes and the Defendant shall obtain and file a transcript of the Judgement [sic] of District Judge (name) in advice [sic] of the hearing."

Where an application for permission is refused on consideration of the papers alone, it is usual for there to be given an opportunity to attend court to renew the application in person. Here though, the judge orders she will be the person who will deal with any oral application; she reserves the case to herself. She has power to do so, but she does not have to do so, and any power must be exercised rationally and judicially. So why does she do this? Her order does not indicate she has any doubts about her decision, notwithstanding the abstract wording ("may"!) used in relation to the £80 costs. To me, in light of my views about her order, this further evidences a determination on her part to defeat the appeal. Mr Smith would be attending an oral hearing with a view to persuading a judge who not only appears to have definitively made up her mind on the issues but has done so with a bemusing lack of regard for the law and natural justice. Do you think that would be a fair and meaningful hearing, or is the failure of the appeal a done deal? And what about the thirty minutes' time limit? Do you think everything could be dealt with in that time (especially, as you will see in the next paragraph, when a transcript of the trial judgment would also fall to be considered)?

Well, if all the above is not bad enough there is one further surprise from the circuit judge. She orders Mr Smith obtain a transcript of the judgment given at the trial. That order is directly contrary to a presumption in the relevant rules that in small claim cases no transcript will be ordered. Rule 52 of the Civil Procedure Rules 1998 deals with "Appeals", and Practice Direction 52B for that rule states at paragraph 6.2: "Except where the claim has been allocated to the small claims track, the appellant must apply for an approved transcript or other record of reasons of the lower court…" Not only does the circuit judge in Mr Smith's case order a transcript, but she orders it for consideration at the permission stage and not merely in readiness for any final appeal hearing.

Obtaining a transcript not only involves work, it involves money; it has to be paid for. There is nothing in the circuit judge's order, or in the appeal which I had drafted, to suggest a transcript was required in this case and, especially, at the permission stage. Bear in mind, Roger Jones Ltd. had not yet responded to the appeal. Maybe in due course, if permission were granted, the company's response would raise an issue pointing to the helpfulness of a transcript, but who could say?

So why does the judge order a transcript, contrary to the presumption in the rules? Why does she not explain how it will help her and why she needs it at the permission stage (after all, her decision does not admit to any doubt as to her views)? Why does she think the case unusual enough to require consideration of a transcript of the trial judgment yet only allocate thirty minutes for the hearing? Or is it just a device employed by her to deter Mr Smith from taking the matter any further? How can she decide that the appeal has no real prospects of success yet think a transcript might help her?

The way forward

There was no doubt in my mind that the circuit judge had ignored the law, illegitimately blocked Mr Smith's appeal and any oral hearing before her would be a complete and utter waste of time and money.

The law is such that, where permission to appeal is refused in a small claim, there is no further right of appeal. If such a case proceeds to a full appeal hearing, there is the right to appeal to the Court of Appeal if the case raises a point of general importance (i.e. one that would affect decisions in other cases now or in the future), but when permission is refused, it's the end of the road.

So, an oral hearing before the circuit judge seemed costly and bound to fail, and there was no further right of appeal. My initial view was there was nothing could be done.

I showed a professional friend who works in the property field that part of the appeal which dealt with the "but for" principle. After reading it, he simply looked at me and said, "There must be something you can do about this." His comment captured the outrage which I felt about the conduct of both the trial judge and the appeal judge, yet I could not see there was anything to be done, and time was ticking because the circuit judge's order gave us seven days only in which to request an oral hearing.

For me, the case had now gone beyond the original matter in dispute between Roger Jones Ltd. and Mr Smith. It had become a case about the integrity of the judges and their accountability. I spent some time on the Internet researching the law, and I found a case[1] which sets out a principle which is common sense: when Parliament gave us the right of appeal, it intended that such an appeal should be a fair process. An appeal which is an unfair process is no appeal at all, and an appeal where a judge has deliberately ignored the law and her duty is a sham[2]. That

---

1   See Gregory & Another v Turner & Another [2003] 1 WLR 1149 citing R (Sivasubramaniam) v Wandsworth County Court [2002] All ER (D) 431.

2   See also Anisminic Ltd v Foreign Compensation Commission [1969] 2 AC 147, which allows a judicial review of any decision which is wrong in law, even where further appeal is prohibited, providing that judicial review itself is not barred by statute. A decision which is wrong in law is a nullity and, therefore, not a valid decision at all.

also seems to accord with Article 6 of the European Convention on Human Rights, which gives the right to a "fair and public hearing... by an independent and impartial tribunal..." Accordingly, I could argue Mr Smith had been unlawfully deprived of the one fair appeal which Parliament intended him to have. Further, I did not think it would be difficult to prove such.

The problem was that such an argument would involve an application to the Administrative Court (a branch of the High Court) in judicial review proceedings, which would involve more cost. Further, you are expected to exhaust all other options before you start a judicial review, i.e. it is a last resort. On the face of it, that meant Mr Smith would have to request the oral hearing offered by the circuit judge.

I spoke with Mr Smith, and I explained the position. Not only would the transcript ordered by the circuit judge have to be paid for but, on the face of it, he would have to attend court for the oral hearing before her, even though both he and I believed that to be a waste of time and money. The court fees and expenses of the judicial review would need to be paid, and the initial fee was £140 (to apply for permission to proceed) with a further £700 due before any final hearing. He asked me if the argument that an appeal had been unfair and, therefore, invalid had ever succeeded before, and I could only tell him I was not aware it had. A day or two later, he sent me a text saying, "You can't beat the system. They'll all stick together." He had decided not to proceed. Naïve fool that I was then, I believed the High Court would have acted to put matters right. I now know differently because, eventually, Mr Smith would place his case before the High Court.

THE HIGH COURT

"A nation that will not enforce its laws has
no claim to the respect and allegiance of its people."

Ambrose Bierce, *Industrial Discontent*

Although Mr Smith had decided not to proceed further with his case, my own fury at what had occurred did not go away, and, in August 2015, I came to believe, rightly or wrongly, that the only plausible explanation for the circuit judge's decision was she and the trial judge had discussed the appeal. Such conduct would be so outrageous a lawyer would hardly dare think it let alone say it. It would amount to a conspiracy to defeat justice and the serious criminal offence of misconduct in public office, and although judges enjoy immunity from prosecution, it is likely that immunity would not apply to such conduct. As everyone knows, an allegation of a crime has to be proved beyond reasonable doubt, and I am not saying the evidence against the two judges is clear enough for that; but Mr Smith's was a civil case, and the standard of proof was the balance of probabilities (the "more likely than not" test). I think it is beyond doubt the circuit judge illegitimately and dishonestly killed off Mr Smith's appeal, and it is more likely than not she conspired with the trial judge to do so.

What led me to believe the judges had talked? Well, certain the circuit judge had dishonestly blocked the appeal, I could only think of two explanations: either, contrary to the clear wording of the rules, she had decided the court should not be wasting time and money on a case which she perceived as being too trivial, or she had wanted to help the trial judge. Even now I cannot think of any other possibility.

The Civil Procedure Rules are very clear that cost is irrelevant to a circuit judge's decision on permission to appeal, and at the beginning of Mr Smith's appeal, I had brought that rule to the judge's attention. Why would a judge deliberately act contrary to that rule? It is not her doing the rule is there, and it is not her money that is being spent in hearing such appeals. It is no skin off her nose to apply the rule. On the contrary, in applying the rule, she would be fulfilling her duty and complying with her oath of office. If she were to break the rule once for this reason, she would break it again and again, and why would a judge needlessly set herself on such an unlawful path for no good reason? It would make no sense at all.

The other possibility, that she had wanted to help the trial judge, introduces the human element and a more personal motive. The trial judge and the circuit judge were both women working out of the same court building. Undoubtedly, they knew one another and participated together in policy meetings at the court. Perhaps they were friends. Perhaps they lunched together from time to time. I then considered again the circuit judge's order where it dealt with costs based on unreasonable behaviour. Why had she even thought of such costs? I thought of all the reasons why her order in that regard was so wrong. I considered the fact that the issue of unreasonable behaviour had arisen at the end of the trial, and I doubted the circuit judge would even have known that since it was not mentioned in the appeal. Was there mention of it in the court file? If so, it would be clear the trial judge had rejected the assertion of unreasonable behaviour – all the more reason for the circuit judge not to have gone there. I also knew there was nothing on the court file to justify such a finding. This part of the judge's order made no sense whatsoever. The ground of appeal which said the trial judge had been wrong to order the £80 legal representative's costs was impossible to deny. It would vex any lawyer to think of a reason to make such an award for those costs in this case, no matter how much it was desired. What the circuit judge had come up with was wholly unsustainable and suspicious by its vagueness ("may"!) and its mention of irrelevant court fees and expenses. It seemed an uncanny coincidence that the issue of unreasonable behaviour had arisen at trial and the circuit judge had, in a manner so at odds with legal principle and the case facts, relied upon such to reject the appeal. I thought of what the trial judge might have wanted to say upon reading the appeal and considered it might be that, although she had not found unreasonable behaviour, nonetheless, the issue had been raised by Miss Brown and, back against the wall, it could be used as a nominal reason for dismissing the appeal. In short, the two judges being colleagues or friends and discussing the appeal was the only possibility that made any sense to me. It explained the circuit judge's motive to deny the appeal and why she had thought to mention costs due to unreasonable behaviour. This was something new for Mr Smith to consider, and when I explained it to him he decided to apply to the High Court for a judicial review of the circuit judge's conduct of the appeal.

There were some obvious difficulties with the judicial review. Firstly, the rule is that if you are unhappy with a decision of a public official or body, you must apply for judicial review as soon as possible and, in any event, no later than three months. However, that time limit can be extended where there is good reason to do so. Secondly, you are expected to exhaust all other options before moving to judicial review, and Mr Smith had not asked for the oral hearing before the circuit judge at which he could have renewed his application for permission to appeal, although, clearly, any option must be a meaningful one of substance and not merely form. Thirdly, I was going to be making unprecedented accusations of misconduct against two of Her Majesty's judges. It was not going to be just another day at the office.

Before applying for judicial review, it is expected you write to the person or body you are unhappy with, setting out in detail your complaint and asking them to put matters right. Six months had already passed since the circuit judge had made her decision, and writing to her would cause more delay, but this was a case where the delay was not of any practical importance, and it was important to write to the judge. On 11th September 2015, in my friend's name and for the attention of the circuit judge, I sent the following email to the Court Manager at the County Court:

"Dear Sir,

I was the Defendant, and then subsequently the Appellant, in the above case. I continue to be advised by Mr Osler, a retired solicitor who acted as my lay representative at the trial and who settled my Grounds of Appeal. It is he who has drafted this e-mail [sic].

Following a finding of liability against me at the trial at (town) on the 26th February 2015 by District Judge (name), an application for permission to appeal was lodged which HHJ (name) refused by order dated the 27th March 2015.

Although some time has passed since HHJ (name) refused permission to appeal on the 27th March 2015, Mr Osler has recently and suddenly come to a realisation that there was a serious irregularity in the appeal process such that it was unfair and should the appeal not be reopened then it is my intention to complain in judicial review proceedings to the Administrative Court with a claim for costs against (name) County Court. I appreciate the 3 months [sic] time limit for bringing such an action has expired but Mr Osler believes there are grounds for extending that time limit pursuant to CPR 3.1(2)(a).

Although the general rule is that there are no further appeals from the appeal judge's decision on an application for permission to appeal (unlike where permission is granted but the appeal fails at the oral hearing when it is then possible to go to the Court of Appeal), there is clear authority that where the application for permission has not been a fair process then the Administrative Court can intervene. This is common sense – if the one appeal given to you by statute was not conducted fairly then effectively you haven't had any appeal as envisaged by Parliament.

Mr Osler believed the Grounds of Appeal to have had a high chance of success and he was surprised when permission was refused on all grounds and could not understand why. There was no point in asking for an oral hearing by way of renewal of the application since the appeal judge seemed emphatic in her decision and had reserved any renewal application to herself. Further, she had ordered there be a transcript of the judgment given at the trial which was a significant cost deterrent for me. In any event, arguments on my behalf had been clearly set out in the written Grounds of Appeal and there was nothing further to add.

Just because Mr Osler strongly disagreed with the appeal decision, that was not a ground for judicial review and so I accepted defeat accepting on its face the order of the appeal judge refusing permission. However, very recently the penny dropped and it has caused Mr Osler to see the appeal process in a different light and to realise how unfair it was.

Ordinarily, the appeal judge would consider the application for permission on the Grounds of Appeal together with the supporting documents and it should not be necessary to consider any other information source in order to understand the decision of the appeal judge. But to understand the decision of HHJ (name) in my case it is necessary to go to another source.

One of the Grounds of Appeal was that the trial judge had allowed the legal representative's costs on the summons (approximately £70) under the fixed costs provisions of Part 45 of the CPR in circumstances which did not allow her to do so. In rejecting this ground, the appeal judge stated that 'Pursuant to CPR r27.14, the District Judge may order one party to pay the Court fees, expenses and further costs if that party has behaved unreasonably'. In the appeal there was no dispute regarding the trial judge's order of court fees or the Claimant's expenses so they were irrelevant. The appeal judge had clearly checked the CPR and concluded that this Ground of Appeal was correct in that the fixed costs provisions of Part 45 did not apply. Instead of just allowing the appeal to proceed on this ground, the appeal judge rejected it, clearly because 'the District Judge may order...further costs if that party has behaved unreasonably' and she substituted the erroneously awarded fixed costs with an award for costs based on my unreasonable behaviour. Effectively, the appeal judge exercised her power to make such order on appeal as the trial judge would have been empowered to make and she made a costs order on the basis that I had behaved unreasonably and she did so at the permission stage and without hearing from the parties.

Apart from any argument that in principle such a power to order costs for unreasonable behaviour would never be used to order fixed costs where they were not allowable, why would the appeal judge, going about her duty without fear or favour, think for a second that there had been unreasonable conduct on my part? It was clear in the Grounds of Appeal that at trial there had been no costs ordered due to unreasonable conduct. The trial judge had simply mistakenly applied the fixed costs provisions. Why was the appeal judge motivated to find a reason for rejecting this ground? There was nothing in the Grounds of Appeal that remotely suggested that there had been unreasonable conduct such that a costs order could have been made on that basis. The appeal judge had not been privy to any representations from the parties regarding costs on the basis of unreasonable conduct.

At trial there had in fact been an application for costs on the basis that my case had been conducted unreasonably (which, incidentally, is strongly denied). The trial judge declined to make such an order but she might if asked suggest that she could have done so had she so wished. Only the trial judge would want to, or could, put forward any basis whatsoever for saying I had been unreasonable. She alone had heard representations on the point and had any information that could be advanced in support of such an assertion. The appeal judge had absolutely no basis for thinking my conduct had been unreasonable. Not unless she had conferred with the trial judge. The only credible explanation for the appeal judge's decision is that the trial judge gave input to the appeal and that of course is highly inappropriate. If I am wrong and the irregularity did not occur then it would assist me greatly if the appeal judge explained what information she relied on in the Grounds of Appeal as allowed her to conclude that I behaved unreasonably such as to justify a costs order in consequence. Such an explanation might ward off any application to the Administrative Court.

Having identified this procedural unfairness, now it is easier to understand the appeal judge's decision to refuse permission on all grounds for it was not an attempt by her to apply the law without fear or favour but rather it was a biased deliberation with the intention of defeating the appeal come what may. Now one sees that the rejection of highly meritorious arguments was but a deliberate ignoring of the facts set out in the Grounds of Appeal and the law. Now one sees that the order for a transcript was but a device intended to deter me from renewing my application for permission at an oral hearing (which it did) – after all, the order seemed unnecessary and unreasonable having regard to the Grounds of Appeal and it was contrary to the presumptions in the CPR which do not envisage a transcript being obtained at any time in an appeal in a small claims track case and even regarding a fast track or multi track case it is not envisaged that a transcript would be obtained until after permission to appeal has been granted. Now now [sic] sees that the refusal at the permission stage was a means of preventing further appeal to the Court of Appeal. Even the mention of irrelevant "Court fees and expenses" in the appeal judge's reasons now looks like a ruse to distract from the true basis of refusal of that ground. I placed my trust in the appeal judge acting fairly. Had my appeal been successful I would have recovered approximately £2,700 including costs.

I paid my £120 court fee for a service, a statutory right of appeal, which I did not receive. The will of Parliament was thwarted.

My complaint is late. The penny just didn't drop until now. The appeal judge intended it should never drop. I assume judges act properly. I do not look for impropriety as a matter of course. Surely that is a correct approach – that one should be slow to think of, or scour for, foul play by our judges. In any event, the unfairness was not transparent and the appeal judge obviously did not intend it to be so. To identify the truth it has been necessary to take into account facts at the trial which were not included in the Grounds of Appeal and which therefore ought to have been irrelevant to the judge's deliberations at the permission stage. Why would I look to understand the appeal judge's decision by considering an irrelevant source not referred to as having been taken into account by her? It would be strange if misconduct by a judge, which through its covertness sought to evade being seen, could defeat a legal challenge on the basis that such a challenge was out of time. That would be perverse.

I request that the appeal is reopened, that a different judge considers afresh the application for permission and that HHJ (name) recuse herself.

This will not prejudice Mr (Jones). When Mr (Jones) first raised his complaint with me there was then a silence of many months before he issued proceedings. I thought his complaint had gone away and then suddenly it raised its head again. It's now just the same for Mr (Jones). He knew I was unhappy with the trial judge's decision and that I had tried to appeal. Further, his solicitors will have copies of all relevant documents or, in the unlikely event they have not, such can be obtained from the court. In any event, the blame for the delay is not mine.

If the appeal judge wishes to deny the assertions in this e-mail [sic] perhaps she will think that the appearance of bias is sufficient to justify the appeal being re-opened. Were she to do this then I would accept at face value her position.

I am conscious that any application to the Administrative Court should be made as soon as possible. Yet the court needs time to consider carefully this e-mail [sic] and also Mr Jones may wish to consult further with his solicitor and make representations. I am sending this on the evening of Friday the 11th September so presumably you won't read it until Monday at the earliest. I ask that you respond by Monday the 28th September at the latest after which Mr Osler will prepare and submit promptly an application for judicial review to the Administrative Court. If you need more time then please let me know with reasons.

If clarification is needed on any part of this e-mail [sic] I will be happy to provide it."

Not having received an acknowledgement of receipt, I sent the email again on 14th September. The court later advised it had not received either of the two emails, and it was necessary to send it again on 29th September, by which time my mother had died and the funeral was to be on 9th October, so I extended the time for a reply to that date.

A copy of the email was sent to Roger Jones Ltd. on 11th September. On 29th September, I asked it to confirm receipt. On 2nd October, I again sent the email to the company asking it to confirm receipt. No reply at any stage was received from the company. In fact, following the trial, the company and Borders Solicitors ignored all correspondence sent to them by me or Mr Smith.

By letter dated 12th October, Mr Smith received the following reply from the court:

"Further to the email of Paul Osler dated the 29th September 2015.

The comments of Her Honour (name) are:

The Court cannot enter into correspondence about the case or re-open the appeal. You may wish to take legal advice."

The assertion that the court cannot enter into correspondence is incorrect. Firstly, it is basic legal knowledge that the human rights law which regulates the fairness of judicial proceedings, unsurprisingly, requires judges give clear and sufficient reasons for their decisions. The request of the judge to explain what information she had relied on in making an order for costs due to unreasonable behaviour was plainly such a request. Secondly, the Civil Procedure Rules include a "Pre-Action Protocol for Judicial Review", which requires a party wishing to complain to the Administrative Court to send a letter to the defendant (the circuit judge) to identify the issues in dispute and establish whether they can be narrowed or litigation avoided – such was my email to the judge. Under the heading "The letter of response", the protocol also says: "Defendants should normally respond within 14 days using the standard format at Annex B. Failure to do so will be taken into account by the court and sanctions may be imposed unless there are good reasons." The failure by the judge to give an explanation for her decision raised the obvious inference she did not have one.

The consequences of the judicial review were potentially serious for the circuit judge. If it succeeded, not only would that be humiliating, but she would have to be removed from office. Even if it failed due to the proceedings having been brought out of time or because Mr Smith had not availed himself of the oral hearing offered, that would not determine the issue as to whether she had breached her duty, and she would still face being removed. The invitation to reopen the appeal was an invitation to her to find a way of correcting the problem without the need for a judicial review. If the judge felt herself in a bind, I wanted her to know that if she could find a way of reopening the matter, difficult though that would be for her, I would not seek my pound of flesh. It is right it would not do for there to be a lack of finality with a judge's decision – we cannot have judges willy-nilly changing their minds and their decisions since the uncertainty would be intolerable. There are circumstances in which judges can correct errors, but I do not think this is one of them. It was worth a try.

The suggestion to Mr Smith that he was being badly advised, and that my advice as a retired solicitor did not constitute legal advice, was unnecessary, disrespectful, inappropriate and unprofessional – don't you think?

On 15th October, the application for judicial review was sent to the Administrative Court. As with the earlier appeal, a judicial review follows a two-stage process. Firstly, a judge decides whether or not to grant permission for the claim to proceed to a full hearing. Initially, the judge considers the application without a hearing and, if permission is refused, an oral hearing is offered (at which the application for permission can be renewed) unless the judge declares the claim to be "totally without merit", which is not usual, especially when a lawyer ("albeit a retired solicitor in a quasi, if I may say, professional role" – per the trial judge) is involved.

In the judicial review claim, I set out my reasons for accusing the circuit judge of having conducted an appeal which amounted to an unfair process, including the assertion that she had discussed the appeal with the district judge. At the beginning of the claim, in Mr Smith's name, I said:

"Although the reasons given by the judge for her decision are written to appear as if she has tried to apply legal principles to the arguments set out in the appeal, it has become clear to me that her stated reasons were not her true reasons and that in reality she has illegitimately killed off my appeal blocking it from going forward and in so doing she has acted with bias in favour of the trial judge, has discussed the appeal with the trial judge and has deliberately ignored legal principles and the will of Parliament. She has breached her oath of office. Accordingly, my application for permission was not a fair process. It was a sham. This is my complaint."

In fact, it did not matter if I was wrong about the two judges having talked since it would have been sufficient that the circuit judge had breached her duty for whatever reason, known or not. If the two judges had talked, it merely made it more outrageous. The notion that the two judges had talked was important in explaining the delay in seeking a judicial review because it was that notion which eventually had persuaded Mr Smith to act.

I also set out the reasons why it had been reasonable for Mr Smith not to have renewed his application orally before the circuit judge.

Since we were seeking a judicial review almost four months after the three-month time limit, it was necessary to apply for an extension of time. When considering an extension of time, the court considers three issues: is there a reasonable excuse for the delay; what is the damage or prejudice to the third party and the detriment to good administration if time is extended; and does the public interest require the claim should proceed[1]?

---

1   R v Secretary of State for Trade & Industry ex p Greenpeace Ltd. [2000] Env LR 221.

In offering a reasonable excuse for the delay, in essence, I stated:

1. The notion the two judges had talked was important in explaining why the judicial review was brought out of time for it was that belief that had prompted Mr Smith to complain to the High Court. It was the straw that broke the camel's back; it was the trigger; the penny simply did not drop until late; when it did drop, Mr Smith understood more clearly what had occurred.

2. The circuit judge had intended that the penny never should have dropped. Her conduct was not transparent. She had not, of course, said, "In complete contravention of the law and my duty, I am refusing permission to appeal"! Rather, she had sought to obscure what she was doing. The wording of her order was a beard.

3. Further, in trying to understand what had happened it was necessary to look outside the Grounds of Appeal I had sent to the circuit judge and to deduce what might have happened (this is something the High Court judge would later implicitly accept since she too would find no justification within the appeal documents for the circuit judge's costs order). Clearly, that made it more difficult to substantiate a complaint.

4. It was also true that my accusations were based on deductive reasoning and an analysis of the judge's decision, which again made it harder to mount a claim in the High Court for the evidence of misconduct was thus more subtle and elusive than it might otherwise have been.

5. Finally, surely the higher courts would want us to be careful in making accusations such as this against judges. These were extraordinary accusations. Could we really be blamed for having been slow in bringing them?

It was easy to deal with the issue of damage or prejudice to the third party, Roger Jones Ltd. There wasn't any. Allowing the judicial review to proceed might be disappointing, but the company knew of the earlier appeal, and there would be no cost to it as a result of a late judicial review. Further, it had not raised any objections to the proposed judicial review. Nor was there any detriment to good administration – this was an exceptional case and an extension of time could easily be justified as being in the interests of justice.

Likewise, it was easy to deal with the issue of the public interest. How could it not be in the public interest that a wrong such as was asserted against the circuit judge be put right? Surely, if my accusations were valid, any right-thinking member of the public would demand that the wrong be righted?

I highlighted the overriding principle of civil proceedings, namely, that cases be conducted justly and at proportionate cost. If there was merit in my accusations they were, clearly, worth the time and cost of being considered, so the important issue was that this claim for judicial review should be dealt with justly. If my accusations had substance, surely it was just that the High Court should interfere? Surely it would want to? The wrong was so great.

The decision

The decision of the High Court judge was dated 14th April 2016, more than five months after the application for judicial review had been sent to the court. This was simply the first-stage decision on permission to proceed, with the judge considering the written arguments and evidence I had sent to the court. Five months is a very long time in which to make such a decision. Official statistics show the then average time for receiving a decision was two months. So why had it taken five months in Mr Smith's case? What had been going on? At one point, Mr Smith rang the court to ask about the progress of his claim, and he was told the court had made an enquiry of the "other party" and was chasing a reply. Really? Apart from requesting the court file from the County Court, there would be no enquiry to be made, and the County Court has confirmed to me there was no such request. So, what was going on during those five months?

If my accusations were accepted, at least the circuit judge would have to be removed from office, and if the accusation the two judges had talked was accepted, the district judge would have to go too. Only the Lord Chief Justice and the Lord Chancellor acting together can remove a judge from office. So, here there were accusations of the most serious nature being made by a retired solicitor, which, if valid, would necessarily involve the country's most senior judge and a cabinet minister. Clearly, this case would be placed before a very senior judge. Imagine my surprise when the decision of the court came from a deputy High Court judge, the most junior rank amongst High Court judges. A deputy is a temporary, and oft part-time, High Court judge. It is inexplicable that this claim was placed before such a grade of judge.

I have mused as to whether senior judges were involved behind the scenes, acting to achieve a desired outcome, namely, the protection of the image of the judiciary. What do you think? Are we to believe this case took five months and found its way to a junior High Court judge without senior judges being aware and involved?

When it came, this is what the order said:

"Permission is refused; the application is considered to be totally without merit.

Reasons

This claim is bound to fail in the judicial review for the following reasons:

1.   *The claim is out of time. The delay is serious given that the decision of HHJ (name) was made on the 27 March 2015 but the claim was lodged on 16 October 2015, nearly 4 months after expiry of the long-stop period of 3 months.*

The explanation given for the delay (page 14-17) is wholly unsatisfactory, based as it is, in part, on the claimant's contention that he was slow to understand the judge's decision and only 'saw much later all too clearly how unfair it was' and, in part, on pure speculation, that Judge (name) must have discussed her application for permission to appeal with District Judge (name) before making her decision on the application. There is quite simply no basis for the contention that Judge (name) had discussed the case with District Judge (name). Any application at trial for costs due to unreasonable behaviour may well have been recorded on documents on file. I have no hesitation in rejecting the explanation for the serious delay.

2.   *The claimant failed to avail himself of the alternative remedy of requesting an oral hearing before Judge (name). Whatever suspicions he may have harboured about the reasons why Judge (name) reserved the matter to herself, she was unarguably entitled to do so as part of her case management powers.*

3.   *As for the underlying merits of the application for permission to challenge the decision of Judge (name) on the merits, there are none. The challenge is based on speculation, that Judge (name) had discussed the case with District Judge (name). This is once again based on the fact that Judge (name) had referred to the fact that the District Judge could order costs for unreasonable behaviour. There is quite simply no basis for the contention*

that Judge (name) had acted with bias in favour of District Judge (name). There is nothing of any substance in the remaining grounds.

4.   In all of the circumstances, and for the reasons given above, I refuse to exercise my discretion to extend time.

<u>Costs</u>

As the defendant has not filed an Acknowledgement of Service, I make no order as to costs.

BY VIRTUE OF CPR 54.12(7) THE CLAIMANT MAY NOT REQUEST THAT THE DECISION TO REFUSE PERMISSION BE RECONSIDERED AT A HEARING."

One of the consequences of declaring the claim to be totally without merit and, thereby, denying an oral hearing was the case would not find its way into open court and, in particular, the High Court where the press and legal commentators might have taken an interest.

So, there you have it. None of my arguments had substance or merit. By now you might be thinking I must be wrong since three judges have ruled against me, with the circuit judge declaring my arguments had no real prospect of success and the High Court judge declaring them to be totally without merit. It would be easy to be influenced by the emphatic nature of the judges' comments and by the status of the judges, yet none of that adds validity to what they said. At every stage, it is necessary to look at what is being said and not by whom and how. We must dare to question. Using reason and evidence, let's have a closer look at this High Court judge's decision.

"The claim is out of time. The delay is serious…"

Here, the judge says the explanation for the delay in bringing the judicial review is insufficient such that the claim is bound to be denied for that reason alone. Although I strongly disagree with that, I do not accuse the judge of breaching her duty or ignoring the law by so ruling. Also, it does not mean my accusations against the district judge and the circuit judge are unfounded, and it still leaves open the possibility of disciplinary action being taken against them.

"The explanation given for the delay (page 14-17) is wholly unsatisfactory, based as it is, in part, on the claimant's contention that he was slow to understand the judge's decision and only 'saw much later all too clearly how unfair it was' and, in part, on pure speculation, that Judge (name) must have discussed his application for permission to appeal with District Judge (name) before making her decision on the application. There is quite simply no basis for the contention that Judge (name) had discussed the case with District Judge (name). Any application at trial for costs due to unreasonable behaviour may well have been recorded on documents on file. I have no hesitation in rejecting the explanation for the serious delay."

Here, the judge repeats her view that the explanation for the delay is unsatisfactory, and she goes on to make two specific points.

The first point is I was slow to see how unfair the circuit judge's decision was, which is to say the idea the two judges talked came to me late. She does not comment on my reasons for having been slow to understand, but, in any event, she thinks it an unacceptable failure on my part. Again, although I strongly disagree, I think it is a view she is entitled to take. Her view cannot be said to be dishonest.

The second point is my assertion that the two judges talked. She says that is pure speculation. That is incorrect. There is a smoking gun, and the evidence and the law lead to my assertion. My analysis of the circuit judge's decision led me to conclude she had illegitimately denied permission to appeal. That was not speculation; it was deductive reasoning and logic based on the case evidence and the law. The smoking gun was the illegitimacy of the circuit judge's decision. Applying the civil standard of proof, namely, the balance of probabilities, to the case facts, led me to believe the judges had talked. Again, that was not pure speculation. Further, the circuit judge failed to respond to the accusation and refused to provide an explanation. There is an element of speculation which combines with deduction, but that is often true in legal cases, including criminal cases where the standard of proof is higher; namely, beyond reasonable doubt.

The High Court judge says there is no basis for my assertion that the judges talked. Is that right? There is basis for saying the circuit judge's decision was dishonest, and the only two reasons I have been able to think of are that she did not think the appeal merited the cost and time or for personal reasons she wanted to help out the district judge. Looking at the nature and failings of her order of costs due to unreasonable behaviour, the fact that at trial such an issue had been raised, the idea that a personal motive is more likely than an impersonal one and applying the test of the balance of probabilities, is there really no basis for saying it is more likely than not the two judges talked?

The High Court judge then makes a statement which I say is wholly inconsistent with the competence required of any lawyer, let alone a judge, and it would lead me to make accusations against this judge of the same nature as those I had made against the circuit judge. The statement is: "Any application for costs due to unreasonable behaviour may well have been recorded on documents on file." With this statement, which seeks to give legitimacy to the circuit judge's order, she dismisses all my criticism of the circuit judge's order that the £80 legal representative's costs be replaced with an order for costs based on unreasonable behaviour. It should be noted the High Court judge clearly accepts there was nothing in the Grounds of Appeal which I had placed before the circuit judge to justify such an order. Rather, she refers to "documents on file". Now, **that** is pure speculation, and it is in favour of the circuit judge. Amongst other things, she ignores the fundamental unfairness in the fact the circuit judge at no stage identified what information she relied on to make her order and in the fact that we were not given an opportunity to make representations before it was made – breaches of natural justice which no right-thinking person would hold to be fair. If this judge really wanted to know whether she had a dishonest circuit judge on her hands, why did she not call for the County Court file to see what was there? The mere fact the circuit judge had refused to explain why she had made the order was sufficient for this argument of the judicial review to have substance. Further, the High Court judge might have been expected to comment on the fact that the circuit judge did not make any costs order but rather used the word "may". This part of the High Court judge's order calls into question her motives and casts doubt on the validity of the whole of her order for it is evidence that, again, there has not been a fair consideration of the arguments. In my opinion, no honest High Court judge could accept as valid that part of the circuit judge's order dealing with the challenge to the £80 fixed costs. To support that part of the circuit judge's order and to dismiss my arguments against it, offends against any just legal procedure and anyone, lawyer or not, who has respect for law.

"The claimant failed to avail himself of the alternative remedy of requesting an oral hearing before Judge (name). Whatever suspicions he may have harboured about the reasons why Judge (name) reserved the matter to herself, she was unarguably entitled to do so as part of her case management powers."

Again, I strongly disagree with this view, but I do not say that of itself it evidences dishonesty. I think it is mistaken. However, it is part of a pattern of all my arguments failing and having no merit.

Whilst it is true a judge can reserve a matter to herself, as with the exercise of all powers, there should be reason for doing so. Power should never be arbitrarily exercised. There was no apparent reason for the circuit judge to reserve the matter to herself, and nor did she give one in explanation. Also, this was not our only reason for not having requested an oral hearing – there was also the issue of the transcript.

Again, this reason for denying the judicial review does not mean the circuit judge or the trial judge should escape disciplinary action for any misconduct on their part.

"As for the underlying merits of the application for permission to challenge the decision of Judge (name) on the merits, there are none. The challenge is again based on speculation, that Judge (name) had discussed the case with District Judge (name). This is once again based on the fact that Judge (name) had referred to the fact that the District Judge could order costs for unreasonable behaviour. There is quite simply no basis for the contention that Judge (name) had acted with bias in favour of District Judge (name). There is nothing of any substance in the remaining grounds."

Here, the judge is saying, putting to one side the issues that the application for judicial review is out of time and that Mr Smith did not request the oral hearing before the circuit judge, my criticism of the circuit judge's decision has no merit. She says the challenge is based on speculation the judges talked. It is true my challenge was, in part, based on that notion (which is far from pure speculation), but it was not the only basis for the challenge. The fundamental basis for the challenge was all the respects in which I was saying the circuit judge's decision was so wrong she must have illegitimately blocked the appeal. Although I went on to accuse the judges of having talked, that was by way of identifying the motive for the circuit judge's illegitimate decision. If the accusation the judges had talked is unjustified, that does not make the circuit judge's decision legitimate or honest. Rather, it simply means there is some other reason for her dishonesty. Essentially, the High Court judge finds anything and everything I have to say is wrong. It follows, this judge thinks to have no merit, amongst other things, my arguments that the circuit judge blatantly ignored the law when assessing whether there was any prospect of success regarding: Mr Smith's liability for the alleged dripping shower; the "but for" principle; the issue of the return of the survey fee; whether the measure of damages was the cost of repairs or diminution in value (in regard to which the circuit judge had ignored two Court of Appeal decisions); whether the test of Mr Smith's liability was whether the company had acted reasonably in light of Mr Turner's complaint; and the validity of the £80 legal representative's costs. According to her, all my criticisms of the circuit judge set out in the previous chapter are without foundation.

It is interesting to note the language employed by the High Court judge and the lengths she goes to in disparaging all my arguments. She could just dismiss the application on the basis it is out of time, yet she appears to be at pains to say that nothing I have said has substance or merit. The explanation for the delay is not just unsatisfactory, rather, it is "wholly" so; my speculation is "pure"; there is "quite simply" no basis for my contention; she has "no hesitation" in rejecting my explanation; the circuit judge was not merely entitled to reserve the matter to herself but she was "unarguably" entitled to do so; as to the merits of any argument, "there are none"; there is "nothing of any substance". It brings to mind the expression: "The lady protests too much, methinks"[2]!

Having regard to all you have read so far, do you think the High Court acted fairly and honestly, or did it act to protect the judges and the image and reputation of the judiciary?

This was the second time fees had been paid to a court in expectation of the law being fairly applied.

---

2   *Hamlet* (3.2.232) by William Shakespeare.

THE JUDICIAL CONDUCT INVESTIGATIONS OFFICE PART ONE

"Laws made by common consent
must not be trampled on by individuals."

Thomas Jefferson, *letter to Colonel Van Meter*

It was my opinion the deputy High Court judge, like the circuit judge before her, had acted dishonestly. Even though some of my points raised in the judicial review had been arguable, none was totally without merit, and some were full of merit. Further, parts of her decision were plainly wrong and inconsistent with the basic competence which can be assumed of such a judge. What had gone on? My opinion was the judge had simply ignored the law and acted to prevent the appeal going further and coming into public view; she had acted dishonestly to defeat justice, protecting her fellow judges and their image;

and she had not just dismissed the appeal, she had crushed it unlawfully.

John Smith could have appealed the deputy High Court judge's decision (to a judge of the Court of Appeal), and the application for permission for a judicial review would have been considered afresh on the papers. However, by then, even I had lost all confidence in the system, and I did not believe such an appeal would be dealt with fairly. In fact, rightly or wrongly, I believed a Court of Appeal judge was waiting for such an appeal, ready to stop it going any further. It can also be said that whilst a further appeal would have given Mr Smith a second bite of the cherry, that did not alter the fact that he had not had a fair first bite of the cherry as was his entitlement. Also, this further appeal had to be lodged within seven days of receiving the deputy High Court judge's order, and it would have cost more money. Due to travel plans, I could not prepare the application within the seven days, and, in any event, John Smith had had enough! He did not appeal further.

However, I decided to make a complaint of misconduct against the deputy High Court judge. This can be done within three months of the conduct complained of. When a judge deliberately breaches her oath of office and, therefore, her duty, and when she ignores the law and acts to defeat justice, she commits a serious criminal offence, namely, misconduct in public office. But whilst other public officials (a police officer, for example) can be prosecuted for such a crime, judges cannot be because they enjoy immunity from prosecution for acts carried out in the course of their duties. Nonetheless, there are statutory regulations which give you the right to make a complaint about a judge's conduct. Such a complaint is made to the Judicial Conduct Investigations Office (the JCIO). Of course, you cannot simply complain that a judge was mistaken in her decision; you have to complain about the judge's conduct. Since my allegations amounted to the crime of misconduct in public office, and since I was accusing the judge of having acted dishonestly, surely my complaint was one of misconduct? Well, that is certainly common sense, but what do the regulations say? Let's have a look.

The Constitutional Reform Act 2005

Section 115 in Part 4 of The Constitutional Reform Act 2005 authorises the Lord Chief Justice to make regulations for the procedures that are to be followed in "the investigation and determination of allegations by any person of misconduct by judicial office holders". Here then, the word "misconduct" appears in a statute, the most authoritative law known to our land and created by Parliament. Now, statutes are used to define words which Parliament thinks need defining, and, although Section 122 deals with "Interpretation of Part 4", there is no definition of "misconduct". It is an ordinary word of the English language and, on the face of it, requires no further interpretation. If Parliament had wanted to give it a specific restrictive definition, it would have done so. It did not.

The Judicial Discipline (Prescribed Procedures) Regulations 2014

These were made under the authority of Section 115. They were made by the Lord Chief Justice, who, I imagine, is quite an intelligent man and very familiar with the practice of defining words when a meaning different to that of ordinary English is to be applied. In fact, Regulation 2 is entitled "Interpretation", and "complaint" is defined as "a complaint containing an allegation of misconduct by a person holding judicial office or other office". However, "misconduct" is not defined. So, neither Parliament nor the Lord Chief Justice has thought it necessary to define "misconduct".

Regulation 4 creates the JCIO, the office responsible for receiving and processing complaints against judges. In paragraph 4, the JCIO is given power to "provide advice to any person regarding the application and interpretation of these Regulations and any rules made under these Regulations". That is not a power to change the regulations or any rules made under them. Nor is it a power to define words. It is merely a power to advise, and any advice must be consistent with the statutory law, the highest law known to our land.

Regulation 7 authorises the Lord Chief Justice to "make rules about the process to be applied in respect of an allegation of misconduct". In this regard, the regulations refer to a "nominated judge", who is one appointed to deal with complaints and must be of at least the same grade as the judge complained about. Reference is made to an "investigating judge", who is one appointed to investigate a complaint but must be of a higher grade than the judge complained about. In other words, a complaint is not going to be ruled on by the JCIO, which is an administrative office not staffed by lawyers. It is going to be ruled on by a judge.

The Judicial Conduct (Judicial and other office holders) Rules 2014

These were made by the Lord Chief Justice under Regulation 7.

Rule 2 is entitled "Interpretation", and, unsurprisingly, "complaint" has the same definition as in Regulation 2 above. Yet again, "misconduct", a word used frequently, and which is obviously fundamental to the rules, is not defined.

Rule 6 simply says, "A complaint must contain an allegation of misconduct".

Rule 21 sets out circumstances in which the JCIO must dismiss a complaint at the outset. Amongst those is (b), which says, "it is about a judicial decision or judicial case management, and raises no question of misconduct". This is applying Rule 6 to a specific situation so there can be no doubt that if you are complaining about a judge's decision, you have to be alleging misconduct on the part of the judge and not merely saying the judge was wrong in her decision. However, providing you are raising a question of misconduct, you clearly can complain about a judge's decision. If the Lord Chief Justice had intended there could be no complaint about any judicial decision, the words "and raises no question of misconduct" would not be there. This rule is critical to what happened next.

The normal procedure set out in the rules is the judge complained about is given an opportunity to respond, after which the complaint is referred to a nominated judge who decides upon the complaint unless it is "sufficiently serious or complex, or that a detailed investigation is required to establish the facts", in which case the nominated judge will refer it to an investigating judge.

My complaint was about a judicial decision, but it included an allegation of a criminal breach of duty on the part of the deputy High Court judge. The rules allow a complaint about a judicial decision providing misconduct is alleged, and it would seem an affront to common sense to say I was not raising such, which the statutory law has seen fit not to define beyond its ordinary meaning. Good to go. What do you think – was my complaint one of misconduct?

The complaint

I know I have mentioned already that my complaint, which can be read in full in Appendix E, was that the judge was dishonest in her decision-making. However, let me now quote directly from it so that the seriousness of my allegations can be fully appreciated. In it I said:

"It is with great regret that I now feel compelled to complain that **in making her order Ms Justice (name) herself knowingly breached her oath of office by suppressing the application irrespective of its legal merits and by seeking to silence the accusations against the judges.** She did not act without fear or favour. Rather, she acted solely to protect her fellow judges and the image of the judiciary. Such behaviour amounts to misconduct in a public office [sic] albeit the judge enjoys the benefit of judicial immunity and cannot be prosecuted and thus this is not a matter for the police. Nonetheless, this is a complaint about conduct (even if the evidence rests in the judge's decision) and is not simply a complaint that the judge got the law wrong. Rather, it is a complaint that she never tried to get it right. She acted to defeat justice. She was dishonest. Her judgment was carefully crafted to ridicule the accusations and arguments being made."

Over the course of fifteen pages, I then analysed the judge's decision and explained why I considered it to have been dishonest. Does that sound like an allegation of misconduct to you?

The response from the JCIO

In a two-page letter, the JCIO stated:

"... the JCIO is unable to accept your complaint for consideration. This is because it does not contain an allegation of misconduct...

The independence of the judiciary means that judges must be free to make decisions without interference from government officials or even other judges unless they are presiding over the case. For this reason the JCIO cannot comment on the decisions or case management of judges... There are no circumstances in which we can seek to challenge, investigate, vary or overturn the decisions which a judge has made in the course of a hearing...

Having considered the matters you have raised, your complaint refers to Ms Justice (name)'s management and decisions in the case and raises no suggestion of judicial misconduct."

It is a confusing explanation because it fuses together two separate notions. The first is the JCIO's view (completely at odds with Rule 21(b) above) that you cannot complain about a judicial decision. The second is its view that I had not alleged misconduct (its stated reason for rejecting my complaint). Saying, effectively, "Because you cannot complain about a judicial decision, the complaint does not allege misconduct", the JCIO appears to be treating those two notions as if they are connected, the logic for which is not immediately obvious. Even if it were true that you could not complain about a judicial decision, why would that mean the complaint was not one of misconduct? It would be perfectly logical to say, "Although your complaint is one of misconduct, you cannot complain about a judicial decision." Why then is the JCIO saying the complaint is not one of misconduct? Given my complaint is clearly about a judicial decision, and given its (albeit incorrect) interpretation of Rule 21(b) as meaning you cannot complain about any such decision, why has it not simply rejected it for that reason? It is confusing, unexplained and irrational. The JCIO misinterprets Rule 21(b), and no explanation is given as to why my complaint is not about misconduct yet that is the reason given for rejecting it. It's as clear as mud.

In an attempt to understand further the JCIO's position, we can look at the "Supplementary Guidance" published on its website. Paragraph 10 is headed "Guidance to the Rules", the "Rules" being the Judicial Conduct (Judicial and other office holders) Rules 2014 (see above).

Regarding Rule 6 (see above), it says this:

> "The JCIO may only consider a complaint that contains an allegation of misconduct by a judicial or other office holder. Such misconduct relates to the judge's personal behaviour for example: a judge shouting or speaking in a sarcastic manner in court; or misuse of judicial status outside of court. It does not relate to decisions or judgments made by a judge in the course of court proceedings. The only way to challenge such matters is through the appellate process."

Accordingly, the JCIO has, without any lawful authority and for no given reason, added to Rule 6 the words, "Such misconduct relates to the judge's personal behaviour... the appellate process"! Again, it appears to be treating the reasoning for this definition as being linked to its incorrect view that it is not permitted to complain about a judicial decision. Why?

Regarding Rule 21(b), the guidance says this:

> "The constitutional independence of the judiciary means that decisions made by a judicial office holder during the course of proceedings are made without the interference of ministers, officials or other judicial office holders (unless they are considering the matter whilst sitting in their judicial capacity, for example, in an appeal hearing). Judicial decisions include, but are not limited to, the way in which proceedings are managed, disclosure of documents, what evidence should be heard and the judgment or sentence given."

To Rule 21(b), in effect, the JCIO has added the word "therefore" as if it read the complaint must be dismissed if "it is about a judicial decision or judicial case management, and, **therefore**, raises no question of misconduct". The JCIO has no lawful authority to do that, and it is not what the rule says.

Its assertion judges should not be interfered with whilst making decisions during proceedings is undoubtedly correct but is wholly irrelevant to a complaint made after that decision has been made and the proceedings concluded, as here.

So, the JCIO has decided, for reasons that are unclear, that "misconduct" refers only to what it calls "personal behaviour". Even though the governing statute enacted by Parliament and the regulations and rules made by the Lord Chief Justice do not define "misconduct", this office of non-lawyers has, without authority or rational explanation, decided to do so! Further, it has decided that you cannot complain about a judicial decision even though Rule 21(b) clearly says you can, and it appears this is behind its restrictive definition of "misconduct", although it is not clear how. If you take away its mistaken view that you cannot complain about a judicial decision, there is absolutely nothing to give any indication whatsoever as to why the JCIO thinks "misconduct" relates only to personal behaviour. Not great, is it?

Do you think the JCIO's rejection of my complaint is rational?

Do you think the JCIO's rejection of my complaint is clearly explained?

Do you think it is consistent with common sense?

Do you think it is consistent with the statute, the regulations and the rules?

Do you think the views I have expressed have no substance?

THE JUDICIAL APPOINTMENTS AND CONDUCT OMBUDSMAN PART ONE

"It is legal because I wish it."

Louis XIV, *speaking in the Parlement de Paris*

The Judicial Appointments and Conduct Ombudsman (the JACO) has the duty and power to intervene where, on a referral to him, it is clear the JCIO is not dealing with a complaint in accordance with the rules and the prescribed procedure. However, he is not concerned with, and cannot interfere with, the merits of a complaint against a judge, which is a matter for the nominated and investigating judges. Given my view that the JCIO was misapplying the rules and, therefore, not processing my complaint in accordance with the procedure (this is known as "maladministration"), I was able to refer the matter to the ombudsman so he could tell it to treat my complaint as valid.

The ombudsman was Paul Kernaghan CBE, QPM. He has an impressive curriculum vitae, which includes nine years as chief constable of Hampshire Constabulary. With that experience and those initials after his name, he must be an intelligent and honest man, mustn't he? His office has confirmed he personally dealt with my case.

The form on which you make a referral to the ombudsman gives you a box of part of one page in which to set out your complaint, the idea being that should be enough for you to persuade the ombudsman to look into the matter and not to immediately reject it. I referred the matter to him, setting out the interpretation of the law which I have explained above. Upon receiving a referral, the ombudsman decides whether it merits investigation or whether it can be immediately dismissed. He decided my referral could be dismissed out of hand. His report, dated 22nd July 2016, can be found in full in Appendix E, but below are the extracts which set out his decision and findings:

"My decision

I have decided that Mr Osler's complaint does not warrant a full investigation. In reaching this conclusion, I am commenting solely on the process by which the JCIO considered the complaint under the arrangements for dealing with concerns about judicial office holders' personal conduct. I cannot comment on the merits of the JCIO's decision or his case before Ms Justice (name)."

With this statement of his decision, he shows an understanding that he is not concerned with the merits of my complaint against the deputy High Court judge. Good, because he had not been asked to consider them. He confirms he is concerned only with the process. Great – me too! At no point had I asked him to consider the merits of my complaint, which would be for the nominated and investigating judges to determine. The JCIO did not make any decision on the merits of my complaint.

He says he cannot comment on the merits of the JCIO's decision. What does he think he should comment on then? He is being asked to review the JCIO's decision to reject my complaint as invalid, which is the only decision made by it and one of process and, therefore, one he can and must consider. So what decision of the JCIO does he have in mind as one he cannot consider? Bizarre!

Also, he talks about "the arrangements for dealing with concerns about judicial office holders' personal conduct", but no such arrangements exist – the arrangements deal with "misconduct" not "personal conduct", and the issue as to whether the former means the latter is fundamental to my complaint about the decision of the JCIO!

Are these errors consistent with the competence required for his office and duties? Is he trying to confuse and mislead?

In the covering letter accompanying his report, he stated:

> "I have now completed a preliminary investigation into your complaint and I enclose a copy of my report. I do not believe a review is necessary as there is no prospect of any finding of maladministration.
>
> I realise that this will be a disappointment to you, but would like to assure you that I considered both the handling of your complaint and the points you raised most carefully."

So, he thinks my referral to him is complete rubbish not warranting further investigation and having "no prospect" of succeeding. He does not need to obtain the opinion of a government lawyer. No, he thinks the JCIO's decision is plainly correct and that I have not got the first idea of what I am talking about. His view contrasts with mine that the JCIO's rejection of my complaint was irrational, unexplained, contrary to the statutory law and without lawful authority. Let's look at his findings to see if he is being rational and honest.

"My findings

I have considered the points Mr Osler raised in order to determine whether his complaint falls within my remit to investigate and my view is that the JCIO handled Mr Osler's complaint properly and correctly and the decision was consistent with the legislation as set in the Judicial Conduct (Judicial and other office holders) Rules 2014 and the appropriate guidance.

The JCIO's view that the issues raised by Mr Osler related to Ms Justice (name)'s judicial decision-making and case management and not her personal conduct was consistent with its guidance. Leaflet JCIO1 on the JCIO website states that:

'A Judge's role in court is to make independent decisions about cases and their management. These are often tough decisions, and Judges have to be firm and direct in the management of their cases. Examples of Judges' decisions include the length or type of sentence, whether a claim can proceed to trial, whether or not a claimant succeeds in their claim, what costs should be awarded and what evidence should be heard.'

'This sort of decision cannot form the subject of a complaint. If you are unhappy with such a decision you are advised to seek legal advice from a solicitor, local law centre, Citizens Advice Bureau or the Community Legal Service to discuss whether you have the right of appeal.'

'If your complaint is not about a Judge's decision but about the Judge's personal conduct you have the right to complain to the JCIO. Examples of potential personal misconduct would be the use of insulting, racist or sexist language.'

The JCIO clearly explained why Ms Justice (name)'s decisions did not relate to her judicial conduct and appropriately advised Mr Osler that these concerns could only be addressed via the appeal process.

I can see no substance in Mr Osler's claim that the JCIO failed to carry out the appropriate investigations into his complaint, in accordance with the Judicial Conduct (Judicial and other office holders) Rules 2014. They properly advised Mr Osler that his complaint did not contain an allegation of misconduct on the part of a named judicial office holder and so, did not meet the criteria set out under Rule 8 of the complaint rules for his complaint to be considered valid. This decision was made following an initial evaluation of the complaints raised by Mr Osler and I can see no issue with the JCIO's handling of his complaint.

Mr Osler correctly points out that Rule 21(b) of the Judicial Conduct (Judicial and other office holders) Rules 2014 only enables the JCIO to dismiss complaints if they are about judicial decisions or judicial case management and they do not raise a question of misconduct. This indicates that complaints about judicial decisions and judicial case management can be considered if there was evidence of misconduct in the decision. However, Mr Osler has provided no evidence that this occurred in this case, therefore, there was no requirement for the JCIO to investigate his complaint further.

I do not believe that Mr Osler has provided me with any examples of maladministration in respect of how the JCIO failed to investigate his complaint properly and, in accordance with Section 110(3) of the Constitutional Reform Act 2005, I do not consider that a review is necessary."

Is all that clear to you? Do not worry if it is not because it is practically unintelligible and, you could be forgiven for thinking, intended to be so. The ombudsman's report in its form looks to be a carefully considered deliberation, and he talks authoritatively with apparently weighty and learned phrases, and he refers to guidance and the statutory law; however, in its substance, it is to all intents and purposes contradictory, irrational, unexplained and without foundation. Let's analyse it.

"I have considered the points Mr Osler raised in order to determine whether his complaint falls within my remit to investigate and my view is that the JCIO handled Mr Osler's complaint properly and correctly and the decision was consistent with the legislation as set in the Judicial Conduct (Judicial and other office holders) Rules 2014 and the appropriate guidance."

Here, he repeats his view that my referral to him is without merit and the JCIO's decision to reject my complaint about the deputy High Court judge was proper and correct. He then says its decision was consistent with legislation. That is manifestly untrue. Firstly, in so far as the JCIO believes you cannot complain about any judicial decision, it is completely at odds with Rule 21(b). Later in his report, the ombudsman expressly states that you can complain about a judicial decision, so he must believe the JCIO is wrong in its interpretation (where is the "proper and correct" in that?). Secondly, the JCIO's treatment of "misconduct" as referring only to personal behaviour is inconsistent with the statutory law in so far as the latter does not define "misconduct" let alone give the definition used by the JCIO. On both counts, the JCIO's views are inconsistent with the legislation and all the more so when you consider its definition of "misconduct" seems to be linked to its erroneous view that you cannot complain about a judicial decision (a view which the ombudsman finds to be wrong). So why is the ombudsman saying this? If he is an intelligent and honest man, why?

As to following "appropriate guidance", he repeats that assertion immediately:

"The JCIO's view that the issues raised by Mr Osler related to Ms (name)'s judicial decision-making and case management and not her personal conduct was consistent with its guidance. Leaflet JCI01 on the JCIO website states that:

'A Judge's role in court is to make independent decisions about cases and their management. These are often tough decisions, and Judges have to be firm and direct in the management of their cases. Examples of Judges' decisions include the length or type of sentence, whether a claim can proceed to trial, whether or not a claimant succeeds in their claim, what costs should be awarded and what evidence should be heard.'

'This sort of decision cannot form the subject of a complaint. If you are unhappy with such a decision you are advised to seek legal advice from a solicitor, local law centre, Citizens Advice Bureau or the Community Legal Service to discuss whether you have the right to appeal.'

'If your complaint is not about a Judge's decision but about the Judge's personal conduct you have the

right to complain to the JCIO. Examples of potential personal misconduct would be the use of insulting, racist or sexist language.'"

There are a number of points to be made here:

1. That the JCIO's view is consistent with its guidance is not really surprising, is it? It would be surprising if it were not. The ombudsman is effectively saying the JCIO is following its own opinion! The JCIO's view and its guidance are one and the same, yet the ombudsman is saying the view is correct because of the guidance. It's nonsensical. He might just as well say the guidance is correct because of the view! This is the mathematical equivalent of A = A. The ombudsman wants to make it A ∴ A, which is not logically possible!

2. In so far as he is implying the JCIO was obliged to follow the guidance that too is nonsensical given the guidance is that of the JCIO and not of a higher authority which it must obey.

3. He uses the word "guidance" as if it has some magical quality which gives it authority; it hasn't. The important question is whether the guidance is correct. You could call it the Fifth Gospel and it would not be any the better for it. The ombudsman's duty is to supervise the JCIO's application of the rules governing complaints against judges, and when a referral is made to him that means he has to decide whether the JCIO's view and its guidance are correct. He seems to be saying here that simply because it bears the title "guidance" it is more likely to be correct and not a matter for his scrutiny. Is he blowing smoke?

4. So, what does he tell us about the correctness of the JCIO's view and its guidance? Without questioning its

correctness, he approvingly cites from one of the JCIO's leaflets to the effect that you cannot complain about a judicial decision and "misconduct" relates to personal behaviour only. However, later in his report, he says you can complain about a judicial decision, so why is he here contradicting himself? Why is he promoting guidance which he later finds to be wrong? Why is he not critically assessing it? His acceptance of "misconduct" as relating only to personal misconduct is wholly unexplained, yet that is the main point in dispute, since it was the reason for the JCIO's decision.

5. In determining the correct procedure to be followed by the JCIO, it is the statutory law which is all important. The ombudsman prefers to steer away from that when he cites the JCIO's guidance instead.

"The JCIO clearly explained why Ms Justice (name)'s decisions did not relate to her judicial conduct and appropriately advised Mr Osler that these concerns could only be addressed via the appeal process."

By "judicial conduct" the ombudsman clearly means personal behaviour, and here, without explanation, he is approving the JCIO's definition of "misconduct" as relating only to personal behaviour on the part of the judge. The JCIO's interpretation of "misconduct" is far from clearly explained, and it appears to be based on its view that you cannot complain about a judge's decision, a view which the ombudsman later states to be incorrect. So, by his own finding, the JCIO's reasoning for its definition of "misconduct" is wrong and, therefore, unexplained.

The JCIO did not, and did not need to, explain, clearly or otherwise, why the judge's decisions "did not relate to her judicial conduct" (i.e. personal behaviour) since it was quite obvious they did not. My complaint was not about the judge's personal behaviour – it was about far more serious misconduct. The important point, and one the ombudsman avoids dealing with throughout his report is: "Why was the JCIO right to treat misconduct as being limited to personal behaviour?" The JCIO's reasoning is clearly wrong so the ombudsman must give an alternative, yet he does not.

"I can see no substance in Mr Osler's claim that the JCIO failed to carry out the appropriate investigations into his complaint, in accordance with the Judicial Conduct (Judicial and other office holders) Rules 2014. They properly advised Mr Osler that his complaint did not contain an allegation of misconduct on the part of a named judicial office holder and so, did not meet the criteria set out under Rule 8 of the complaint rules for his complaint to be considered valid. This decision was made following an initial evaluation of the complaints raised by Mr Osler and I can see no issue with the JCIO's handling of his complaint."

So, that abortion of reason which is the JCIO's decision to reject my complaint as invalid is here hailed by the ombudsman as proper advice with which he sees "no issue", and he finds my referral to him has "no substance" even though he later accepts I am correct to say you can complain about a judicial decision (and, by implication, the JCIO was wrong to say otherwise) and even though the statutory law does not limit "misconduct" to personal behaviour.

Impliedly and surreptitiously, for he does not expressly say so, the ombudsman is simply accepting the JCIO's limited definition of "misconduct". He does not explain why. Throughout his report, the idea that "misconduct" relates only to personal behaviour is an assumed truth for him. He does not deal at all with why it should be so. He does not deal with my arguments as to why such a definition is wrong. He does not consider the statutory law relating to it. Yet the JCIO rejected my complaint against the judge for that very reason, which, therefore, is the key point the ombudsman must deal with and explain. Why does he not do so? Why does he write a four-page report which does not deal directly with the key point in dispute but, rather, assumes it to be true? He might just as well have written a report which simply said: "I find 'misconduct' relates only to the personal behaviour of the judge. I am not going to explain why. I am not going to answer Mr Osler's arguments as to why it does not. Although the JCIO's explanation is nonsense, I will pretend otherwise." If you doubt this is what he is doing, set yourself the challenge of working out from his report (see Appendix E) why he treats "misconduct" as relating only to personal behaviour; ask whether he deals with my arguments against that interpretation; note he finds you can complain about a judicial decision, so his reasoning cannot be that of the JCIO; ask whether what he says is helpful or is meaningless waffle which does not deal with the real issue but seeks to distract from it.

"Mr Osler correctly points out that Rule 21(b) of the Judicial Conduct (Judicial and other office holders) Rules 2014 only enables the JCIO to dismiss complaints if they are about judicial decisions or judicial case management, and they do not raise a question of misconduct. This indicates that complaints about judicial decisions and judicial case management can be considered if there was evidence of misconduct in the decision. However, Mr Osler has provided no evidence that this occurred in this case, therefore, there was no requirement for the JCIO to investigate his complaint further.

I do not believe that Mr Osler has provided me with any examples of maladministration in respect

of how the JCIO failed to investigate his complaint properly and, in accordance with Section 110(3) of the Constitutional Reform Act 2005, I do not consider that a review is necessary."

Here then is where the ombudsman accepts my argument that Rule 21(b) means you can complain about a judicial decision. That is no great concession as it is the only sensible interpretation of the rule. What then is the meaning of his previous ramblings seemingly in favour of the JCIO's view in its guidance that you cannot complain about a judge's decision?

He concludes that in my fifteen-page letter of complaint against the deputy High Court judge I have not included an allegation of misconduct. Again, he is accepting that "misconduct" refers only to personal behaviour, but he gives no reason why. The JCIO thinks it is because you cannot complain about a judicial decision, but he holds that view to be wrong, so he cannot rely on that. He does not admit, let alone deal with, the fact that the JCIO's reasoning is wrong – on the contrary, he says it was "clearly explained"!

Summary

By any standards, my complaint against the deputy High Court judge alleges serious misconduct, and it amounts to the criminal offence of misconduct in public office for which people other than judges go to prison. If you look at the ombudsman's report and crystallise out his reason for upholding the JCIO's decision it is simply this: "misconduct" can only refer to a judge's personal behaviour. He does not explain why. He is not direct in stating it. Rather, he ignores the JCIO's flawed reasoning and the arguments I set out against that interpretation, and he fills his report with a summary of mine and the JCIO's position, with illogical, approving waffle (regarding which he later contradicts himself) about the JCIO's guidance and a smattering of references to his duty and the law. He uses phrases such as "consistent with the legislation" and "consistent with its guidance", which appear to give weight to his decision yet are either wrong or meaningless. Essentially, his position is that "misconduct" can only relate to personal behaviour and, seemingly, it is because he wishes it. His duty is to explain why it is so, but he does not – he does not even try.

Given his finding that the JCIO is wrong to think you cannot complain about a judicial decision, and given the JCIO seems to rely on that incorrect view to justify its limited definition of "misconduct", it is surprising he concludes that the JCIO "handled Mr Osler's complaint properly and correctly", that it "clearly explained why Ms Justice (name)'s decisions did not relate to her judicial conduct", that it "appropriately advised Mr Osler these concerns could only be addressed via the appeal process" and that it "properly advised Mr Osler that his complaint did not contain an allegation of misconduct".

One of the points I made in my referral to the ombudsman was if "misconduct" was limited to personal behaviour, there would never be a complaint about a judicial decision, and that would be strange since Rule 21(b) clearly envisages there will be. The kind of personal misconduct the JCIO is thinking of would not affect the correctness or quality of a judge's decision. To affect a decision, the misconduct has to involve bias or an element of dishonesty on the part of the judge. Imagine a judge refers in her decision to a party who is Italian by saying, "This greasy wop asks me to believe…", and she finds against him. That would be racist and disgraceful conduct, but it does not affect the quality of her decision. If you want to complain about the judge's decision, you have to start saying the racism meant she was biased and she did not, therefore, apply the law honestly in accordance with her duty, and that is not the kind of misconduct the JCIO means. The rules say you can complain about a judicial decision, and the ombudsman agrees, and it is inconsistent to say "misconduct" only relates to personal behaviour. Again, the ombudsman does not deal with this argument, and he does not give an example of when a complaint about the personal behaviour of a judge would also be a complaint about a judicial decision within Rule 21(b). Together with my other arguments, he simply decides this point "does not warrant a full investigation", "there is no prospect of any finding of maladministration" and he can "see no substance in Mr Osler's claim".

It is easy for decision-makers to use superlative words and phrases as are mentioned above, yet they are meaningless unless supported by sound reasoning, something which is noticeably absent on the part of the ombudsman.

He does not deal with the fact that neither the statute nor the regulations nor the rules define "misconduct". Apart from accepting that Rule 21(b) means you can complain about a judge's decision, he does not deal with the legislation at all. He does not deal with the fact that the JCIO is not empowered to change, add to, subtract from or overrule the statutory rules. His report is short on specifics and long on generalities. It is a classic example of how to write a lot yet say little, hardly any of which stands up to the most basic scrutiny. Remember, at this stage, he is just deciding whether my referral should be looked into further and, without any meaningful, rational explanation, he dismisses it on the basis I am clearly wrong. In his covering letter, he says he has considered matters "most carefully"!

Do you think the ombudsman's report is consistent with that of an intelligent and honest man holding high office in our country, or is there something of the farm about it? Is he acting to protect the judges?

THE JUDICIAL CONDUCT INVESTIGATIONS OFFICE PART TWO

"Better no law than laws not enforced."

Proverb

When a public official or a government department makes a decision but misapplies the law, the decision can be challenged in judicial review proceedings in the High Court. Both the JCIO and the ombudsman were there to be challenged, and the claim had to be started as soon as possible and, in any event, within three months. Despite my loss of faith in judges, if it could be done cheaply, I was happy to try because it would flush out into open court my allegations against the three judges and maybe people would become interested in what had happened. With that in mind, I decided to write again to the JCIO.

Amongst other things, I asked if it knew of any legal authority to the effect that "misconduct" meant "personal behaviour", or was it claiming its power to advise on the application and interpretation of the regulations and rules (Regulation 4) gave it the power to define "misconduct"? I also explained I wanted to put the matter before a judge, and I suggested we could do that without the use of lawyers, which would keep the costs down. After all, how difficult would it be to let a High Court judge see what I, the JCIO and the ombudsman were saying and for us to receive the view of the court? I pointed out that the JCIO has no vested interest in what the correct interpretation of the rules is, so why would it want to instruct lawyers and rack up costs unnecessarily? What does it care what interpretation it works to as long as it is the correct one backed by the authority of a High Court judge? The response from the JCIO, dated 9th September 2016, was surprising.

Firstly, it confirmed its definition of "misconduct" was an exercise of its power to advise on the application and interpretation of the rules though it did not claim that gave it a power to define words or phrases in the statutory provisions.

In explanation of its definition of "misconduct", it said this:

> "The Judicial Conduct (Judicial and other office holders) Rules 2014 specify the circumstances under which the JCIO must dismiss a complaint (see rule 21(a) to (l)). This includes complaints about judicial decision and case management, which do not constitute matters of misconduct. Therefore, any complaint relating to matters of judicial decision and case management only fall to be rejected as not containing an allegation of misconduct. As misconduct cannot include matters of judicial decision and case management, because these are matters of judicial function, misconduct must be personal on the part of the office holder."

Wow! So, if there had been any doubt before about the reasoning of the JCIO, there was none now. It had been spelt out. Its reason for defining "misconduct" as personal behaviour is because it can have no other meaning if you cannot complain about a judge's decision. This was new information because, apart from confirming the link, it explained why it was connecting its definition of "misconduct" with its notion that you cannot complain about a judicial decision. But hang on, isn't the effect of Rule 21(b) that you can complain about a judge's decision, and didn't the ombudsman agree? So, the JCIO is ignoring the ombudsman's finding on that point (why?), and its error is the reasoning behind its definition of "misconduct"! What of the ombudsman's claims that the JCIO had clearly explained its reasons, that it had handled my complaint properly and correctly in a manner consistent with the legislation and that my arguments had no substance, no prospects and did not warrant further investigation? The JCIO's reasoning is obviously fallacious and wholly misconceived, based as it is on a fundamental error. It was clear from the JCIO's initial rejection of my complaint that it was misinterpreting Rule 21(b) by wrongly thinking you can never complain about a judicial decision, and it was pretty clear that was behind its definition of "misconduct", but it had not explained why that was so. Now it was crystal clear. It had confirmed and explained the link, and it was plainly wrong, even by the ombudsman's findings.

The ombudsman would have to look at this again and concede that the JCIO had erred, wouldn't he? After all, in the logic from the JCIO reading "A therefore B", he had decided A (you cannot complain about a judicial decision) was wrong, in which case the JCIO's reasoning as to why B ("misconduct" can only relate to a judge's personal behaviour) was true must be wrong in his eyes. That is not a difficult concept, is it? And the ombudsman is a former chief constable, so he must be a stickler for the law, mustn't he? And these blokes only get CBEs and QPMs because of their ability, service and integrity, don't they? He would have to look at this again and either change his decision or give an explanation different to that of the JCIO as to why "misconduct" is limited to a judge's personal behaviour. Although in his report he avoided recognising and criticising what, even at that stage, was clearly flawed reasoning given by the JCIO, and, without explanation or directness, he treated the JCIO's definition of "misconduct" as the law, its further explanation now set out in its letter of 9th September was so starkly wrong surely he would have to accept that fact, deal with it head on and give an explanation as to why he was upholding their decision, i.e. tell us why misconduct is limited to personal behaviour.

Secondly, the JCIO declined my offer of low-cost, straightforward court proceedings and, instead, advised it "contests any claim in full" (even though it must have known its fundamental reasoning had, effectively, been found to be wrong by the ombudsman) and the proceedings should be sent to the Treasury Solicitor's Department. Well, it is taxpayers' money after all. Why should the JCIO worry?! Who are these people there to serve?

THE JUDICIAL APPOINTMENTS AND CONDUCT OMBUDSMAN PART TWO

"The final test of civilization of a people
is the respect they have for law."

Lewis F. Korns, *Thoughts*

In light of the JCIO's clarification of its flawed reasoning, I decided to write to the ombudsman and ask him to revisit his decision. Since I had new and relevant information to present to him, which showed the JCIO to be wrong beyond any doubt in its explanation as to why "misconduct" should be limited to personal behaviour, it was clearly proper for me to write to him again. By email dated 12th September 2016, I wrote the following:

"My above complaint related to a decision of the JCIO to treat a complaint made to them against Deputy High Court Judge (name) as being invalid. In a decision dated the 22nd July, Mr Kernaghan ruled in favour of the JCIO.

Subsequent to Mr Kernaghan's decision and in contemplation of a judicial review, I wrote to the JCIO asking if they could either refer me to any legal authority to the effect that 'misconduct' means 'personal misconduct' or confirm that they were so defining it in exercise of powers given to them to issue guidance on interpretation. Their answer is such that, had it been known to Mr Kernaghan, it would surely have led to him finding against the JCIO. We are all under an obligation to reconsider our views so that unnecessary judicial reviews can be avoided and I wonder would Mr Kernaghan be prepared to revisit his decision.

The JCIO's answer to my question is that the rules are such that **ANY** complaint about a judicial decision is prohibited and 'As misconduct cannot include matters of judicial decision and case management, because these are matters of judicial function, misconduct must be personal on the part of the office holder'. In other words, their logic for defining 'misconduct' as 'personal misconduct' is founded on the notion that one can never complain about a judicial decision. Mr Kernaghan accepted that notion was incorrect and, seeing that it has erroneously led to the JCIO treating 'misconduct' as 'personal misconduct', he would surely now hold that to be an error – the very foundation of the JCIO's reasoning is something Mr Kernaghan found to be wrong!"

The ombudsman responded by letter dated 26th September 2016, saying:

143

"Thank you for your email, dated 12 September 2016, with attached response to your proposed claim for judicial review, dated 9 September 2016, from the Judicial Conduct Investigations Office (JCIO). I note the points you raise and your request that I revisit my decision on your complaint, as set out in my report to you, dated 22 July 2016.

My remit was to consider the process by which the JCIO handled your complaint about Ms Justice (name). I cannot comment on or review the decisions made by the JCIO during their investigation. Having reconsidered the correspondence on this complaint, it is my view that the JCIO's assessment that your concerns related to judicial decisions or case management was consistent with guidance. The JCIO could not review the merits of Ms Justice (name)'s decisions and there was no evidence of misconduct that the JCIO could consider. In addition, the JCIO clearly explained why the judicial decisions made by Ms Justice (name) in the course of your case did not relate to judicial misconduct.

Therefore, there was no requirement for the JCIO to investigate your complaint further and there was no evidence of maladministration in the JCIO's investigation process. I understand your disappointment that your complaint has not been resolved as you would wish, but I must now bring our correspondence to a close."

So, instead of thanking me for drawing his attention to the new information from the JCIO, which confirmed beyond doubt its erroneous reasoning, he gets slightly shirty telling me he "must now bring our correspondence to a close"!

Firstly, he explains his remit was "to consider the process by which the JCIO handled your complaint" and he "cannot comment on or review the decisions made by the JCIO during

144

their investigation". Well, he had only been asked to consider the process and at no stage had he been asked to comment on or review an investigative decision by the JCIO. In fact, the JCIO did not investigate my complaint at all since it treated it as invalid and refused to process it. Why then is he saying this? In any event, he said this in his report. Why is he not dealing with the new information provided to him?

Secondly, once again he asserts that the JCIO's assessment that my complaint related to judicial decisions or case management was consistent with guidance. Well, I had not claimed my complaint did not relate to a judicial decision (the very opposite was true). I had simply claimed you can complain about a judicial decision providing the complaint raises an issue of misconduct (and mine clearly did). In his report, he had agreed with that proposition (why does it not bother him that the JCIO in its reasoning is continuing to misinterpret Rule 21 b) and, to that extent, is ignoring his ruling?). Has he changed his mind? Why the contradiction? Why does he think it matters that my complaint is about a judicial decision? Also, he's again referring to this guidance. The whole point of my complaint is that the guidance is wrong. You don't answer a complaint against the JCIO by saying its own guidance says it is right – that is to allow it to be judge and jury in its own cause! The question is whether the guidance is correct, and in his report, he had found it to be wrong in saying you cannot complain about a judicial decision. Again, he is just repeating his initial report. Why is he not dealing with the new information?

Thirdly, he says the JCIO could not review the merits of the deputy High Court judge's decisions. Well, given he accepted that one can complain about a judicial decision, how does he think that is going to work without any consideration of the merits of that decision? The point of my complaint against the judge was that the lack of merit in her decision was such it could only be explained by dishonesty on her part, i.e. misconduct. The regulations and rules do not say you cannot complain about the merits of a decision – they only require the complaint raises an issue of misconduct. If the merits of a judge's decision evidence misconduct, the complaint is made out, and it will be a judge who makes that assessment. This point is not to be confused with the fact that the ombudsman does not consider the merits of a complaint against a judge when assessing whether the JCIO has followed a correct process. Anyway, why is he still not dealing with the new information?

Fourthly, he says there was no evidence of misconduct (by "evidence" he means allegation) that the JCIO could consider. That is true only if the JCIO's definition of "misconduct" as personal behaviour is correct (his assumed truth), and he now has before him clear evidence its reasoning in that regard is mistaken. Again, he said all this in his report. Why is he not dealing with the new information? Why is he sticking with the erroneous definition of "misconduct"? Why does he not admit the JCIO is wrong in that regard? Why does he not tell us why "misconduct" is limited to a judge's personal behaviour?

Finally, he repeats the idea that the JCIO has "clearly explained" why the judge's decisions did not relate to misconduct. He is just repeating what he said in his initial report and going round in circles. He has totally ignored the new information presented to him and prefers to talk in riddles about judicial decisions and misconduct. He is being irrational. He appears to want to dodge the real issue and to blow smoke in defence of the JCIO. He makes out my difficulty with his decision is not based on sound reasoning but, rather, on an inability to accept disappointment. He refuses to deal with the false reasoning of the JCIO and the fact there is no explanation given as to why "misconduct" relates only to personal behaviour. Remember, at this stage he is just being asked to accept the matter is worthy of being looked into further. He is adamant such is not necessary – all is clear; the JCIO is correct; you cannot complain about a judicial decision; then again, you can; misconduct relates only to personal behaviour; but he does not say why; fairies dance on rainbows at midnight; oranges are nuts because lemons cannot grow in Italy; A = A; A ❖ B; not A ❖ B; 2 + 2 = 5!

If, deliberately, he has ignored the law, acted with bias and breached his duty to ensure the JCIO follows the statutory provisions, he is guilty of the crime of misconduct in public office, but, unlike the judges, he is not immune from prosecution. What do you think he has done?

THE MPs AND THE MINISTRY OF JUSTICE

"I reverence the law, but not where it is a
pretext for wrong, which it should be the
very object of law to hinder... I hold it blasphemy
to say that a man ought not to fight against authority:
there is no great religion and no great freedom
that has not done it."

George Eliot, *Felix Holt*

The rights to have the law justly applied and to fair appeals and complaints are given to us by our chief lawmaker, Parliament. It was my opinion I had clear evidence three judges had blatantly ignored the law and thwarted those rights in Mr Smith's case. Further, they had been assisted in that by the incompetence, if not the dishonesty, of the JCIO and the ombudsman. Mr Smith's case evidenced a systemic problem with the behaviour of judges and officials and their accountability. I wrote to my MP.

By email dated 2nd August 2016, I set out my concerns for the attention of Mrs Lucy Frazer QC, MP (Conservative). At the end of the email I said:

> "In summary, I am a retired solicitor informing you that I have a case which evidences that three judges have acted with bias, ignored the law and dishonestly defeated justice. In so doing, they have defied the rule of law (see Bingham's sixth principle), the *Magna Carta* ("to no one will we deny right or justice"), the criminal law (misconduct in public office), the civil law (negligence and general principles of causation and loss), statutory rules (the Civil Procedure Rules) and their oath of office. They cannot be prosecuted. They have ignored the will of Parliament and denied one of Her Majesty's subjects his rights, knowingly causing him harm. The JCIO and the ombudsman won't even recognise the validity of the complaint. I invite you to look at this case. I am happy to discuss it with you in person or in correspondence. Are you interested? If so, I will make the documents available to you…"

By letter dated 3rd August, she replied:

> "… it appears that you have already pursued the legitimate avenues to challenge judicial decisions and it is, therefore, difficult to see what further steps can be taken.
>
> I will, however, write to the Minister for Courts and Justice, Sir Oliver Heald, to share your concerns and see if he has any further thoughts or ideas on the matters you raise."

I thought this a negative response, and I feared she was just passing the buck and simply wanting to be seen to do something.

It seemed to be lost on her that when the "legitimate avenues" are manifestly not functioning lawfully, perhaps Parliament should have a look at them.

Subsequently, by letter dated 13th September 2016, she forwarded to me a letter to her from Dr Phillip Lee MP (Conservative) of the Ministry of Justice. It said:

> "Thank you for your letter of 3 August 2016 on behalf of your constituent, Mr Paul Osler of (address), regarding allegations of criminal dishonesty on the part of three judges. I am responding on behalf of my colleague, as I am the duty minister during this recess.
>
> The Lord Chief Justice and the Lord Chancellor are jointly responsible for matters relating to judicial conduct and discipline. Their responsibilities cover matters relating to allegations of potential personal misconduct in the way a judicial office holder has behaved, whether inside or outside the courtroom. Their remit does not extend to considering matters relating to judicial decision and case management, including the application of the law. Complaints about judicial misconduct are handled in accordance with the provisions of the Judicial Discipline (Prescribed Procedures) Regulations 2014 and supporting rules. They are assisted in their duty by the Judicial Conduct Investigation Office (JCIO).
>
> I note that Mr Osler's complaint was considered by the JCIO and a letter was sent to him on 28 June 2016 explaining that the matters he raised related to judicial decision and case management. This decision has also been upheld by the Judicial Appointments and Conduct Ombudsman. The Lord Chancellor and Lord Chief Justice have no powers to review the decisions judges make or intervene in individual cases. Judges carry

out their duties having regard only to the facts and arguments which are brought before them, and it is their task to apply the law in that light. Judicial decisions are for Judges and Judges alone. They are not answerable for their decisions in the same way a government minister is. A judge's decision may only be challenged by the parties to a case by way of an appeal or, in some circumstances, by judicial review.

I am sorry that I am unable to assist Mr Osler with his concerns in regard to this case."

It is a letter written with confidence and apparent authority as to the law, but is it right?

The first thing to note is he sees complaints against judges as being limited to "personal misconduct" when, as I have explained, there is no lawful basis for that. This is one of the errors the JCIO has propagated, and it appears Dr Lee is basing his letter on its views.

Secondly, he is relying on another error propagated by the JCIO, namely, its view that it is not possible to make a complaint about a judicial decision. In this regard, he is not only contradicted by the statutory rules, which say a person can complain "about a judicial decision", but also by the ombudsman in his report, in which he said, "This indicates that complaints can be considered if there is evidence of misconduct in the decision."

There are two further things worthy of note, and they are of great concern:

1. He seems to have great faith judges do no wrong: "Judges carry out their duties having regard only to the facts and arguments which are brought before them..." That is what they ought to do, but is it what they do? A retired solicitor is claiming to have evidence of

dishonest decision-making by three judges, and he is not interested in properly investigating that fact. Rather, he seems to assume I must be wrong.

2. He believes judges should not be supervised in their decision-making: "Judicial decisions are for Judges and Judges alone. They are not answerable for their decisions in the same way a government minister is." Although according to the law, namely Rule 21(b), he is wrong that a judge's decision cannot be looked at in a complaint of misconduct, in practice he is right, because we know the JCIO and the ombudsman will unlawfully prevent such.

If nothing else, his letter is testament to the fact that judges are accountable only to judges (even if it were allowed to proceed, a complaint of misconduct about a judge's decision would be dealt with by a judge), and they are not (pursuant to the law created by the JCIO and the ombudsman, which, apparently, has precedence over the law enacted by our sovereign Parliament) accountable to anyone, including Parliament, for any dishonesty in their decision-making. Is that situation good enough? Whilst an appeal might put right a judge's dishonest decision, that depends on the honesty of the appeal judge(s), and they cannot all be trusted, as Mr Smith's case shows. Further, even if an appeal is successful, the offending judges are not disciplined in any way for their dishonesty.

Finally, regarding Dr Lee's letter, you can see someone has looked into my complaint to the JCIO for he refers to the JCIO's letter to me dated 28th June, which I had not mentioned in my email to Mrs Frazer. Neither the JCIO officers nor the ombudsman are qualified lawyers, so why has the Ministry of Justice accepted their views over mine? The matter is obviously important, so why has it not been referred to a senior government lawyer for it to be thoroughly investigated?

When forwarding a copy of Dr Lee's letter to me, Mrs Frazer waved the white flag, ending:

"Please do let me know if you think there might be anything else that I can do for you within my role as an MP."

By letter dated 21st September, I wrote again to Mrs Frazer, and I explained why I considered the legal position adopted by the JCIO, the ombudsman and Dr Lee to be incorrect, and I enclosed the copy correspondence with the JCIO and the ombudsman. At this point, I did not have the final letter from the ombudsman dated 26th September, but I made her aware I was awaiting his response, and that, if he were honest, he would have to change his decision. I ended my email saying:

"Even if my complaint now moves forward, it will be dealt with by judges, which brings me back to the fact that judges collectively are above the law. I do not accept that MPs, Ministers and Parliament are unable to confront judges when they are plainly abusing their powers and depriving us of rights given to us by Parliament. A complaint to the JCIO is but one path to the disciplining of a judge. The 'rights of the individual' are oft lauded yet they only exist when they do not conflict with the ultimate power holders. Per se, the individual is powerless. In China they neither have the form nor the substance of justice. Here we are cleverer because we have the form but, when it suits and those with power can get away with it, we lack the substance."

Then I received the ombudsman's letter dated 26th September, and I forwarded a copy to Mrs Frazer pointing out the absurdity of it. I also commented that, if in her last letter to me dated 13th September she was inferring I was seeking her help in a capacity other than that of MP, I was not. In a response dated 17th October, she ended our correspondence with the following words:

"As the Ombudsman has already considered your case, I am not sure how best I can assist. This is primarily a legal matter, as I am sure you are aware. If you think that there is something I can do as your MP, please do let me know as I would be happy to assist."

Although I had presented her with evidence which raised serious concerns about the integrity of the ombudsman, let alone the error of his decision, she was happy to do nothing. Either she felt powerless, or she was disinterested. She was clearly of the view that legal matters are not ones for the attention of MPs. Hang on! Have I not said Parliament is our chief lawmaker and its will is sovereign? Almost everything an MP touches involves the law. And was she saying systemic dishonesty by judges, and those who are involved in their supervision, is not a matter of interest to MPs? Why did she not fight to have this matter thoroughly looked into? She could not have cared less[1].

---

1   I also wrote to the Labour Party about this case and it did not respond. On 9th January 2018 Lucy Frazer was appointed Parliamentary Under Secretary at the Ministry of Justice.

SO WHAT? WHO CARES?

"All that is necessary for the triumph
of evil is that good men do nothing."

Edmund Burke (attributed to)

Lack of integrity

If the judges in Mr Smith's case have behaved dishonestly, so what? Does it matter in a relatively insignificant case, such as that of Mr Smith's, if judges act contrary to the law, flagrantly breaching their oath of office, depriving a citizen of his or her rights, cheating them out of their hard-earned money and thwarting the will of our elected Parliament? Does it matter if our civil servants betray us and act to protect those in power? Does it matter if our MPs do not care and do nothing? A cynic might say, "Grow up; it's a corrupt world; accept it; you cannot change it." It might though be said that dishonesty in minor cases, if unchecked, sows the seeds of dishonesty in greater cases. In any event, is not the dishonesty the same irrespective of the gravity of the case? If a judge is prepared to act dishonestly in a minor case, how much more willing will she be to so act in a serious case? Most people would lie to avoid going to prison, but fewer, perhaps, would lie to save a fiver. If you would lie to save a fiver, would you hesitate to lie to avoid prison? And if a series of three judges at different levels of the judicial hierarchy were involved, does not Mr Smith's case evidence a systemic dishonesty? Perhaps the seriousness of Mr Smith's case is greater than its monetary value indicates.

Also, the importance of a case is relative. A case worth £2,000 might not mean much to an MP, but it can mean a great deal to an unemployed widow with a disabled child. Whilst we might understand that there needs to be an intelligent use of our country's money, that is not an excuse for allowing our judges and public officials to abuse their power and act contrary to the law. I am not saying our system of civil justice is fundamentally wrong in its design; I am saying the rules are not being applied properly and we need to make judges more accountable for their abuses.

Some might say judges are, at times, entitled to abuse their power for the greater good. In Mr Smith's case, such an argument might be employed to justify any failure by the High Court to take action against the district judge and the circuit judge so that a positive public image of the judiciary could be maintained. This idea is not new. In Shakespeare's *Merchant of Venice*, to prevent Shylock having his pound of flesh from Antonio, Bassanio urges the judge:

> "And I beseech you,
> Wrest once the law to your authority:
> To do a great right, do a little wrong,
> And curb this devil of his will."

But Portia, the acting judge, replies:

"It must not be. There is no power in Venice
Can alter a decree established:
'T will be recorded for a precedent,
And many an error, by the same example,
Will rush into the state. It cannot be."

It cannot be; it would become a precedent. It must never be that we turn a blind eye to abuse of power by judges – where would be the control over them, and where would be the certainty that good law requires? We must speak out. Acceptance leads to attitudes such as "look after number one" and "get the other person before he gets you", and we become the very person we despise. It allows a cancer to grow unchecked. We must demand change. We must remove judges who deliberately defeat justice, imprison civil servants who blatantly act contrary to their duty and vote out the MPs who do not care.

Does not the conduct of the judges in Mr Smith's case evidence a staggering hypocrisy? Think of those the judges have sent to prison for acting to defeat justice – the MPs Jonathan Aitken and Chris Huhne (who, unlike judges, were not charged with a duty of administering justice) immediately spring to mind, but there are many examples. If I am right in my accusations against the judges in Mr Smith's case, it is one rule for them and another for everyone else.

Lord Neuberger, then President of The Supreme Court, on 26th August 2014, in a speech about the rule of law given at the Hong Kong Correspondents' Club said:

"It is self-evident that if judges are dishonest, if the judges can be bribed or suborned, the rule of law will be fatally undermined. If judges break the law, what possible hope is there that anyone else will bother to observe it? Similarly, competence and fairness are essential requirements of a judge. An incompetent or unfair judge is almost as much of a contradiction in terms as a dishonest judge. Competence is a prerequisite for judicial office. So is fairness, which involves judges making sure that the law is applied equally and in the same way irrespective of the means, gender, age and other characteristics. It is why justice is traditionally portrayed in western art as blind."

Fine words; but where's the action? Was the circuit judge blind to the fact that a fellow judge was being criticised in the appeal? Was the High Court judge blind to the fact that two judges and the image of the judiciary were under attack in the judicial review? When the behaviour of the judges in Mr Smith's case is considered, the words of Lord Neuberger just look like judicial propaganda.

Lack of accountability

We must dispel the myth that our judges are accountable. Let us have a look at some statements from government websites regarding accountability:

> "We have stated that judges who commit a criminal offence may be subject to an investigation by the Office for Judicial Complaints…" *The principles of judicial accountability*, Courts and Tribunals Judiciary website.

In Mr Smith's case, I accused the High Court judge of a criminal offence; namely, misconduct in public office, yet my complaint was declared invalid. Further, on the Judicial Conduct Investigations Office website, under the question "What can I complain about?", it is said:

> "We cannot investigate… allegations of criminal activity… (criminal allegations should be directed to the police)."

Well, which is it – can they or can't they investigate a criminal offence? The position of the JCIO is yet another error on its part. It is not in the statutory law that it cannot investigate a criminal allegation, and it is common sense that it may wish to do so prior to referring a matter to the police. Also, there are circumstances where a prosecution would not be possible, but a complaint to the JCIO would be. For example, where it is clear the evidence is not sufficient to prove the matter beyond reasonable doubt, and a prosecution is therefore not viable, disciplinary action via a complaint to the JCIO would still be possible since the test would be the balance of probabilities, i.e. is it more likely than not the judge committed this wrong? Another example is that in the performance of their duties judges are immune from prosecution for criminal activity, but they are not immune from a complaint of misconduct (although the current situation, as I have set out, is that the JCIO and the ombudsman are not applying the law to that end). It is illogical for the JCIO to maintain it cannot investigate criminal activity by a judge.

On the Courts and Tribunals Judiciary website, it is said judges are subject to a "considerable degree of accountability". Hmm, let's see: judges enjoy an immunity from prosecution for acts in the performance of their duties; cannot be sued; cannot be complained about unless they have been rude or misused their status (the law according to the JCIO and the ombudsman!); and can have another judge overturn their decisions on appeal (should the second judge be honest enough to do so, but this would not discipline the first judge for any misconduct). Where's the accountability? Oh yes, if a judge is rude!

On the judiciary.gov website can be found a paper entitled "The Accountability of the Judiciary", issued by the Judiciary of England and Wales. Under the heading "The accountability of individual judges", four possible bases of accountability are considered:

1. Under "Accountability to the executive of the state", it is explained a judge can be disciplined or removed if the Lord Chief Justice and the Lord Chancellor agree. So, the alleged misconduct has to get to their attention in the first place (my allegation against the High Court judge could not even get itself treated as one of misconduct), and the Lord Chief Justice, a judge, can block it.

2. Under "Accountability to the legislative branch of the state", the bottom line is, in theory, a judge of the High Court or the Court of Appeal can be removed by Parliament, but this is accompanied by the comment, "It has not been exercised in modern history"! Odd, isn't it, that Mrs Lucy Frazer QC, MP did not even consider the issues raised by Mr Smith's case to be a matter for her as an MP?

3. There is then "Internal accountability to 'the judiciary'", which means judges supervising judges through appeals, but it comes with the caveat that "… one of the guarantees of independence under Article 6 of the European Convention on Human Rights, reflecting underlying common law principle, is that judges must be free from outside instructions or pressure from other members of the court or the judiciary. This limits the extent and form of discipline to which a judge may be subjected."

4. The fourth type of accountability mentioned is "Accountability to the public", by which it is meant the media can scrutinise judges' decisions and comment upon them. Under this heading, it is also pointed out that, "Complaints against the personal conduct of the judiciary (other than against decisions in proceedings) are handled by the Office for Judicial Complaints" and "Complaints about the handling of such complaints can be made to the Judicial Appointments and Conduct

Ombudsman" (there are those "personal conduct" and judicial decision limitations again – what happened to the statutory law and Rule 21(b)?!). So, as long as a judge sticks it to you politely, that's ok!

All this amounts to is, through appeals, judges supervise judges' decisions (but not conduct, and only if you're lucky enough to get an honest appeal judge), a complaint can be made about a judge who is rude and the media can criticise if they wish. Big deal! How about judges not having immunity and being accountable for their dishonest and criminal conduct in the performance of their duties? How about judges not just being accountable to other judges? How about judges being sent to prison like everyone else when the misconduct demands it?

I wrote to the Judicial Office asking it to direct me to any legal authority which limited misconduct to a judge's personal conduct, and I pointed out that Rule 21(b) permitted a complaint about a judge's decision. I have not received a reply.

Article 6 of the European Convention on Human Rights is referred to in point three, above. The right to a fair trial before an independent tribunal is a right given to **us**, not to judges, but here it is used to justify a lack of accountability for judges. Here it is used to protect them, not us. Article 6 means we are entitled to have an unbiased judge who, at the time of presiding over our case, is free from outside influence and pressure. It does not mean judges should not be held to account for their behaviour after the case is finished and following a proper inquiry. Were the judges in Mr Smith's case independent and unbiased? Allowing judges to do what they please without holding them to account appears in Mr Smith's case to have encouraged the opposite to the independence promised to us by Article 6!

There is a fifth heading which could be added to the above list. Although judges enjoy immunity from prosecution, it is not absolute. There are circumstances in which they can be prosecuted. Judges only enjoy immunity for acts in the performance of their judicial function. It is probable, therefore, if a judge conspired with another to defeat justice, she would not enjoy immunity. Examples might include a judge accepting a bribe to throw a case, or two or more judges illegitimately discussing a case out of court with a view to thwarting justice. The difficulty would be obtaining the evidence to sustain a prosecution. If, however, a judge, without the involvement of others, threw a case because she wanted to protect a colleague or the image of the judiciary, she would not lose immunity, yet the material difference between that and accepting a bribe is motive, not the deliberate and criminal breach of duty.

Following the Brexit challenge in the Supreme Court, Lord Neuberger expressed some concern with the press criticism of the judges of that case, alleging that some of it undermined the rule of law. To be fair, he was not discouraging criticism but, rightly, called for it to be responsible. He said that undermining the judiciary without good reason risked undermining our society and, therefore, the rule of law of which judges are "the ultimate guardians" (try telling the latter to Mr Smith!). Yet surely it is a failure to freely criticise judges and to deal with their misconduct which undermines the rule of law? Whether the criticism (which should always seek to be responsible) is with good reason or not, it is healthy for it to be aired and for people to make their own minds up. No criticism of judges undermines the rule of law. If it is without good reason, irresponsible and unjustified, the people should be trusted to see it for what it is. It is a case such as Mr Smith's which undermines the rule of law.

"In an age of universal deceit,
telling the truth is a revolutionary act."

George Orwell (attributed to)

APPENDIX A: Some of the evidence before the trial judge.

a) Letter dated 19th October 2012 from Roger Jones to Mr Turner, refuting the latter's complaint.

Our Ref.: ███████████

19ᵗʰ October 2012

Mr ████████████

Dear Sir

Without Prejudice – ████████████████████

I refer to ██████████ letters dated 26ᵗʰ September 2012 and 12ᵗʰ October 2012, and your emails dated 2ⁿᵈ and 14ᵗʰ October 2012.

In view of the concluding comments of your most recent email I feel it is appropriate for me to formally write to you to clarify matters as we see them and to make my firms' position fundamentally clear.

████████████ undertook a Level 2 (RICS Homebuyers Survey and Valuation) survey of the above property on Monday 13ᵗʰ August 2012. You were fully aware of the scope and limitations of the survey as you signed our Conditions of Engagement (which are RICS Standard Terms of Engagement) on 4ᵗʰ August 2012.

Page 6 of the Conditions of Engagement outlines the Condition Ratings. As stated in both of ██████████ previous letters, the Conservatory was given an overall Condition rating of 3 (Defects that are serious and/or need to be repaired, replaced or investigated urgently). Therefore, the condition of the conservatory should have been investigated further, i.e., inspected by builders and formal quotations for repairs obtained. Page 23 of the report is entitled "What to do now". It clearly states that you should get at least two quotations from experienced contractors who are properly insured. It also states that you should get the contractors to put the quotations in writing.

The wording of our report reads "The timber framed conservatory requires a number of repairs including the replacement of defective double glazed seals and defective flashings and roof liners". Therefore, the estimates that you obtained should have covered the majority of the roof issues. As stated in previous correspondence, the decay to the roof timbers that you mention is repairable, and should not be expensive. The cost of the repairs to the conservatory roof timbers should not affect the value and saleability of the property in any way. However, as a gesture of goodwill, and without any admission of liability, I am prepared to consider meeting the reasonable cost of repairs to the defective timbers which are outlined on page 1 of ████████ letter dated 26ᵗʰ September 2012. Please arrange for a quotation to be sent for our consideration. I reserve the right to obtain additional quotations for comparison purposes.

You have made reference to evidence of a previous fire which occurred within the roof space. ████ has confirmed in his letter dated 12th October 2012 that there is no damage to the roof timbers. Therefore, this would not be reported within the scope of a RICS Homebuyers Survey and Valuation.

As ████ stated in his letter dated 12th October 2012, there was no dripping from the shower unit at the time of inspection. In any event this would not have been reported within the scope of a RICS Homebuyers Survey and Valuation. I draw your attention to Page 4 of our Conditions of Engagement which states "The surveyor will not carry out specialist tests or assess the efficiency of electrical, gas, plumbing and heating or drainage installations (or whether they meet current regulations) or the inside of any chimney, boiler or other flue".

I note your intention to make a formal complaint to the RICS. I have therefore reviewed the file and I am satisfied that the survey was carried out for you in a proper manner in accordance with the RICS Standard Terms of Engagement. These terms were sent to you and returned signed to us, which provided proof that you had read and understood fully how we would undertake the survey of the property. It fully explains the condition ratings and the actions that are necessary on your part. I will rigorously defend any allegations that we have not acted in a proper manner or in accordance with the RICS Standard Terms of Engagement.

I also note your attention to pursue a claim through the small claims court. I will again rigorously defend any allegations that we have not acted in a proper manner or in accordance with the RICS Standard Terms of Engagement. I reserve the right to seek to recover any reasonable costs incurred by us in defending your allegations.

As I see it the main bone of contention is the rot to the conservatory timbers for which, I am, as stated, as a gesture of goodwill, and without any admission of liability, prepared to consider meeting the reasonable cost of in order to bring a conclusion to this matter.

Yours faithfully

P.P.

████ BSc (Hons) MRICS MBEng
Registered RICS Valuer

b) Email dated 14th January 2013 from Mr Turner to Roger Jones, asserting the bathroom "cost £200 to repair".

From:
Sent:  @tiscali.co.uk>
To: 14 January 2013 13:57
Subject: RE:

It is disappointing but not surprising for complaints of a firm's work to be treated rather dismissively but your offer of £925 when I have already paid you £425 does not even meet [redacted] own estimate of £600 for the work to be done.

As a consequence of this and in order to make sure I have understood the full extent of the omissions I have been obtaining further costings and have had some of the urgent work done.

As initailly outlined the omissions are (with my latest comment in bold):

1. The Homebuyer survey draws attention to the need for a number of repairs E7including the replacement of defective double glazed seals and deflective flashings and roof liners.'
It makes no reference to any of the internal problems – one of the supporting beams is completely rotten, has moved and is held up by a philips screw. (Photo attached.). Both cross beams are also rotten and have been extensively repaired. There are no proper downpipes from the roof – three copper tubes of about ¾ inch diameter are used and are clearly not fit for purpose. The roof leaks chronically in at least four places.

I have detailed costing to repair the conservatory roof and replacing the rotten timbers comes to around £600/700 as part of an overall cost of £4000

2. The main roof
There has clearly been a fire in the loft space at some time but there is no reference to it.

You may wish to have the roof inspected as this was clearly not done by [redacted] the roof has clearly been fire damaged and replacing it will cost £3636 plus vat £4363. If this had been drawn to my attention before the purchase the price would have been reduced by this amount.

3. Downstairs Bathroom
There is no apparent reference to this room but the shower unit drips non stop from the control unit and will need the tiles to be removed and for it to be replaced. It is almost a flow of water and has clearly been going on for a while.

This cost £200 to repair.

The cost of the repairs to the roof are substantially higher than anticipated.

Total cost to me of your survey

Survey	425
Conservatory	650
Roof	4000
Bathroom	200
Total	5275

I would welcome your comments and an appreciation that vat is a cost to me even though it is not to you.

Regards
[redacted]

c) Property Ombudsman's summary of Mr Turner's complaint, showing, inter alia, £200 for the bathroom.

ABOUT YOUR COMPLAINT   CASE REF: ▓▓▓▓

Homebuyers Survey/Valuation   Survey and valuation

Mr▓▓▓▓ has a complaint with ▓▓▓▓▓▓▓▓ and he has provided the following issues to be investigated:

- The Homebuyer survey draws attention to the need for a number of repairs - E7 - including the replacement of defective double glazed seals and deflective flashings and roof liners. It makes no reference to any of the internal problems.
- One of the supporting beams is completely rotten; has moved and is held up by a Philips screw.
- Both cross beams are also rotten and have been extensively repaired.
- There are no proper downpipes from the roof. Three copper tubes are used and are clearly not fit for purpose. The roof leaks chronically in at least four places.
- The main roof: There has clearly been a fire in the loft space at some time but there is no reference to it. The roof has clearly been fire damaged and needs replacing.
- Downstairs Bathroom: There is no apparent reference to this room but the shower unit drips non stop from the control unit and will need the tiles to be removed and for it to be replaced. It is almost a flow of water and has clearly been going on for a while.

The complaint has been escalated in writing and a deadlock letter dated 21 January 2013 has been received.

As a resolution to the complaint, Mr▓▓▓▓ is seeking financial recompense to carry out the following works required and for the reimbursement of the survey fee:

- Survey - £425
- Conservatory - £650
- Roof - £4000
- Bathroom - £200
(alawson)

DO NOT FORGET:
- We will decide as soon as possible whether your complaint is within our Terms of Reference and whether we can deal with it. We will let you know as quickly as we can.
- Include copies of all relevant papers regarding the complaint. The Ombudsman can only make a decision based upon the evidence presented for investigation.
- Quote your unique Case Reference number on all documents.
- Sign and return one copy, keeping the other for your files – you will need this for your Case Reference number.
- If you believe that some information should be kept confidential between you and us, you should mark that information clearly and tell us why you think we should not pass it to the other party. We will consider your request – but we may not agree to it, unless there is a strong case for confidentiality, such as security reasons.

Please investigate my complaint. I am happy for you to share any information I provide to you with the firm.

By signing this form I also give permission for the firm to release to you any information they hold about me or my Complaint which may be relevant to your investigation.

166

d) Letter dated 22nd February 2013 from Roger Jones to the Property Ombudsman, refuting Mr Turner's claim.

Our Ref.: ████████

Your Case Ref.: ██████

22nd February 2013

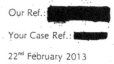

Investigation Officer
Ombudsman Services: Property
PO Box 1021
Warrington
WA4 9FE

Dear Mr█████

Without Prejudice – Mr ██████████████████████████

I refer to your emailed correspondence dated 14th February 2013.

My opinion on the facts of the case and the items referred to by Mr █████ are as follows:

With regard to the conservatory, it was given a Condition Rating of 3 in the report which indicates that "the defects are serious and/or need to be repaired, replaced or investigated urgently". Under the "What to do now – Getting quotations" section of the Home Buyers Report, it states that "before you make a legal commitment to buy the property, you should get reports and quotations for all the repairs".

We have not been supplied with any documentation or estimates by Mr █████ to suggest that he followed the advice contained within the report. Had he done this, the repairs to the conservatory would have been known to him prior to purchase.

With regard to the fire damage within the roof space, my letter dated 19th October 2012 to ████████ confirms that there is no resultant structural damage to the timbers and would therefore not be reported within the scope of a RICS Homebuyers Survey and Valuation. The inspecting surveyor has also confirmed that the main roof covering itself was in good condition at the time of inspection and was performing satisfactorily (apparently it was re-roofed with new slates fairly recently). We have received no third party documentation or evidence from Mr █████ to substantiate his claims regarding the condition of the roof.

With regard to the dripping shower unit, the inspecting surveyor confirmed in his letter dated 12th October 2012 to Mr █████ that there was no dripping from the shower unit at the time of inspection and in any event this would not have been reported within the scope of a RICS Homebuyers Survey and Valuation.

We were alerted to the complaint by a telephone call from Mr █████ on Wednesday 19th September 2012, and the inspecting surveyor,

FRICS, inspected the following day to assess Mr █████ complaint and respond accordingly, which he did by way of a letter dated 26th September 2012.

I have enclosed for your consideration copies of all relevant documentation which has been sent to or received from Mr █████ since, which I have collated in chronological order so that you can see the way we have responded to the queries raised by the client.

I would also add, as I consider it relevant, that there has been considerable disparity in Mr █████ monetary claims, none of which has been supported by any third party evidence. His email dated 2nd October 2012 suggested £8,000 - £12,000. This was followed by his email dated 14th October 2012 which suggested £5,000. His subsequent email dated 21st October 2012 suggested that he ould "settle" for £2,500. This was followed by his email dated 23rd October 20. confirming that he will "settle" for £1,425. His email dated 14th January 2013 now suggests £5,275. As stated, I can confirm that at no stage have we received any supporting or third party evidence to verify any of Mr █████ claims.

As requested, I enclose evidence to demonstrate the service that was to be provided to Mr █████ and that he understood the contract. This is in the form of our Conditions of Engagement which were signed by Mr █████ on 4th August 2012 (copy enclosed).

I confirm that the fee charged to the client was £425-00 including VAT.

As requested, I enclose a copy of the inspecting site notes, photographs, and the RICS Homebuyers' Report dated 15th August 2012.

I also enclose as requested, a copy of our complaint handling procedure.

I hope that from the supporting evidence I have supplied you will see that the survey was carried out for the client out in a proper manner in accordance with the RICS Standard Terms of Engagement. These terms were sent to Mr █████ and returned signed to us, which provided proof he had understood fully how the survey would be undertaken. It fully explains the purpose and scope of the survey, the condition ratings, and the actions that are necessary on the part of the client.

I will be happy to assist you further in your investigation. To this end if you require any further information, or if you have any queries, please do not hesitate to contact me.

Yours sincerely

█████ BSc (Hons) MRICS MBEng
Registered RICS Valuer

E: █████ b.uk

Encl

e) Mr Turner's County Court claim, showing £354 for the bathroom.

Claim Form

In the	
	NORTHAMPTON (CCBC)
	County Court
Claim No.	▓▓▓▓▓▓▓
Issue Date	▓▓▓▓▓▓

Claimant

Court Address   MCOL

MONEY CLAIM ONLINE
NORTHAMPTON COUNTY COURT
21-27 ST KATHARINE'S STREET
NORTHAMPTON
NN1 2LH

Court telephone number: 0845 6015935

Address for sending documents and payments (if different)

Defendant

Defendant

3614

Particulars of Claim

▓▓▓▓▓ Co were commissioned to undertake a survey of a property which I was buying-▓▓▓▓▓▓The survey was not done properly and they offered to refund the payment I had made to them for the survey - #425 and a goodwill payment of #500 to do the work which they agreed needed to be done.
The claim was originally fairly complicated. Tis is a more limited claim. Before proceeding to Court I went to the Ombudsman but he would not deal with two final elements of my claim:
1. Although #500 would correct the narrow works outlined it did not take into #100 vat.2. Plumbing work of #354 was rejected because I did not have evidence. I now have statement from previous owner and an invoice. The claimant claims interest under section 69 of the County Courts Act 1984 at the rate of 8% a year from 02/11/2012 to 20/08/2013 on #1,379.00 and also interest at the same rate up to the date of judgment or earlier payment at a daily rate of #0.30.

The Claimant believes that the facts stated in this claim form are true and I am duly authorised by the claimant to sign this statement

signed ▓▓▓▓▓
(Claimant)(Claimant's Solicitor)
XXXXXXXXXXXXXXX

N1CPC Claim form (06.12)

Important Note

- You have a limited time in which to reply to this claim form

- Please read all the guidance notes on the back of this form - they set out the time limits and tell you what you can do about the claim

- You can respond to this claim online. Log on to www.moneyclaim.gov.uk

- You will need the claim number (see above) and the following password wxwPdRX5

	£
Amount claimed	1379.00
Court fee	70.00
Solicitor's costs	0.00
Total amount	1449.00

14453

APPENDIX B: The district judge's order made at trial on 26th February 2015.

General Form of Judgment or Order

In the County Court at ▮▮▮▮▮	
Claim Number	▮▮▮▮▮
Date	4 March 2015

▮▮▮▮▮ & CO LTD	1st Claimant Ref
▮▮▮▮▮	1st Defendant Ref

Before District Judge ▮▮▮▮▮ sitting at the County Court at ▮▮▮▮▮ sitting at the ▮▮▮▮▮ ▮▮▮▮▮▮▮▮▮▮

Upon hearing Counsel for the Claimant and the Claimant in person and the Defendant in person.

IT IS ORDERED THAT

There be Judgment for the Claimant against the Defendant for £1579.83 for debt and £527.00 for costs. The total of £2106.83 to be paid within 14 days.

Dated 26 February 2015

APPENDIX C: The circuit judge's order of 23rd March 2015, dismissing the appeal, and her letter dated 12th October 2015.

General Form of Judgment or Order

In the County Court at	
Claim Number	██████
Date	27 March 2015

	1st Claimant Ref
████████ & CO LTD	
████████	1st Defendant Ref

Before Her Honour Judge ████████ sitting at the County Court at ████████

Upon considering without a hearing the Defendant's application for permission to appeal the order made by District Judge ████ on 26th February 2015

And upon reading the Defendant's grounds of appeal

IT IS ORDERED THAT

The application is dismissed for the following reasons:

The Defendant has no real prospect of success.

REASONS: - On the evidence, the District Judge was entitled to find that the Defendant breached his duty of care and that the breach caused the Claimants to suffer the loss claimed. The Defendant concedes that the District Judge found his evidence "implausible" and that there were defects which he failed to mention in his report. The District Judge was entitled to prefer the written evidence. Pursuant to CPR r 27.14, the District Judge may order one party to pay the Court fees, expenses, and further costs if that party has behaved unreasonably.

The above ruling having been made without an oral hearing, the Defendant may within 7 days of receipt of this order request such a hearing before His Honour Judge ████████ If the Defendant requests an oral hearing it shall be listed for 30 minutes and the Defendant shall obtain and file a transcript of the Judgement of District Judge ████ in advice of the hearing.

Dated 23 March 2015

 **HM Courts & Tribunals Service**

HM Courts & Tribunals Service
The County Court at

www.gov.uk

Your ref:

12 October 2015

Dear Sir

Re: Case Number: ████████ & Co Ltd v ████████

Further to the email of Paul Osler dated 29 September 2015.

The comments of Her Honour ████████ are;

" The Court cannot enter into correspondence about the case or re-open the appeal. You may wish to take legal advice."

Yours faithfully,

Civil Section

COUNTY COURT ENQUIRIES ████████

172

APPENDIX D: High Court documents.

a) Letter from the Administrative Court, advising the judicial review claim was issued on 3rd November 2015.

**HM Courts &
Tribunals Service**

Administrative Court Office
Royal Courts of Justice
Strand
London
WC2A 2LL

DX 44457 RCJ / Strand

T 020 7947 6655
F 020 7947 6802 / 7845
E administrativecourtoffice.general
office@hmcts.x.gsi.gov.uk

Text Phone 18001 020 7947 6655

www.justice.gov.uk

Our ref: CO/███████
Your ref: In Person

03 November 2015

Dear Sir / Madam,

    <u>Re. The Queen on the application of</u>█████ versus █████**COUNTY
<u>COURT</u>**

Your claim for judicial review has been issued today and was received by the Court on the date noted in the 'Date Filed' field of the sealed claim form.

You will need to serve all documents on the Defendant [and Interested Party/ies]. Please note that service must be effected within 7 days of the date this letter, and a Certificate of Service lodged with the Court. Failure to comply with this requirement may result in the file in these proceedings being closed.

When serving the claim on the Defendant [and any interested party(ies)], please ensure you enclose a copy of attached notice.

Please also note our Case Reference number CO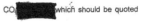which should be quoted whenever you communicate with the Court.

Your attention is drawn to Part 54 of the Civil Procedure Rules and its accompanying Practice Directions, which give guidance on future procedural matters.

      *** IMPORTANT INFORMATION – PLEASE READ ***

Please note that it is the Court's practice to destroy **all** copy documentation and **any** bundles immediately following the conclusion of these proceedings, and to retain original documentation on the Court file. **We therefore strongly advise you to keep copies of any documents that you submit to the Court.**

If you wish to have your copy documentation or bundles returned to you, **you must notify the Court, <u>in writing</u>, at your earliest convenience, and prior to the conclusion of these proceedings,** specifying whether you intend to come to the Court and collect your documentation, or whether you would like the Court to return it to you by post or by DX. Please note that for reasons of cost, the Court will not return documentation by Recorded Delivery or Registered post.

The Administrative Court Office will not accept service via email. When using the above email address it should be noted that mail sent after 4.30 p.m. may not be opened until 9.00 a.m. on the following working day. Court users should not send sensitive information over the public internet.

b) The deputy High Court judge's order dated 14th April 2016.

High Court of Justice
en's Bench Division
ministrative Court

CO Ref: CO███████

★ 14 APR 2016 ★
LONDON

In the matter of an application for Judicial Review

The Queen on the application of ██████████

Claimant

versus

███████County Court

Defendant

Application for permission to apply for Judicial Review
NOTIFICATION of the Judge's decision (CPR Part 54.11, 54.12)

Following consideration of the documents lodged by the Claimant

Order by ██████████ sitting as Deputy High Court Judge

Permission is refused; the application is considered to be totally without merit.

<u>Reasons:</u>

This claim is bound to fail in the judicial review proceedings, for the following reasons:

1. The claim is out of time. The delay is serious, given that the decision of HHJ ██████████ was made on 27 March 2015 but the claim was lodged on 16 October 2015, nearly 4 months after expiry of the long-stop period of 3 months.

   The explanation given for the delay (page 14-17) is wholly unsatisfactory, based as it is, in part, on the claimant's contention that he was slow to understand the judge's decision and only "*saw much later all to clearly how unfair it was*" and, in part, on pure speculation, that Judge ██████████must have discussed his application for permission to appeal with District Judge ████ before making her decision on the application. There is quite simply no basis for the contention that Judge ██████████had discussed the case with District Judge ████ Any application at trial for costs due to unreasonable behaviour may well have been recorded on documents on file. I have no hesitation in rejecting the explanation for the serious delay.

2. The claimant failed to avail himself of the alternative remedy of requesting an oral hearing before Judge ████ ████ Whatever suspicions he may have harboured about the reasons why Judge ██████████reserved the matter to herself, she was unarguably entitled to do so as part of her case management powers.

3. As for the underlying merits of the application for permission to challenge the decision of Judge ██████████ on the merits, there are none. The challenge is again based on speculation, that Judge ██████████had discussed the case with District Judge ████This is once again based on the fact that Judge████ had referred to the fact that the District Judge could order costs for unreasonable behaviour. There is quite simply no basis for the contention that Judge ██████████ had acted with bias in favour of District Judge ████ There is nothing of any substance in the remaining grounds.

4. In all of the circumstances, and for the reasons given above, I refuse to exercise my discretion to extend time.

<u>Costs:</u>

As the defendant has not filed an Acknowledgement of Service, I make no order as to costs.

BY VIRTUE OF CPR 54.12(7) THE CLAIMANT MAY NOT REQUEST THAT THE DECISION TO REFUSE PERMISSION BE RECONSIDERED AT A HEARING.

Signed:

The date of service of this order is calculated from the date in the section below

Form JR15 v. MAY 2015 Judicial Review Permission Refused AS TOTALLY WITHOUT MERIT [NLA *claim issued on or after 1 July 2013*]

c) Civil Justice Statistics Quarterly, showing the mean time between the lodging of a claim and a decision on permission to have been sixty-seven days in 2015 and sixty-four in 2016 (contains public sector information licensed under the Open Government Licence v3.0.).

Table 2.3

Index

Timeliness[1] (in days) of Judicial Review[2,5] cases started between 2000-2016 by stage reached

Year	Case lodged to permission decision (only cases granted or refused)		Case lodged to oral renewal decision (only cases granted or refused)		Case lodged to final hearing decision (only cases found in favour of appellant or defendant)	
	Number of cases	Mean timeliness in days[1,3]	Number of cases	Mean timeliness in days[1,3]	Number of cases	Mean timeliness in days[1,3]
2000	3,201	65	659	137	823	205
2001	3,773	62	1142	129	612	191
2002	4,178	65	1090	130	389	219
2003	4,203	62	1027	117	374	197
2004	2,747	60	740	134	314	241
2005	3,495	78	817	209	369	278
2006	3,960	118	897	266	430	425
2007	4,184	114	979	267	406	356
2008	4,364	89	1109	180	382	338
2009	4,975	111	1178	214	454	310
2010	6,185	89	1370	256	462	334
2011	6,627	95	1517	224	470	387
2012	7,775	111	1959	234	498	397
2013[4]	8,229	126	1130	216	506	374
2014	3,131	77	483	161	367	270
2015	3,578	67	462	143	297	227
2016	2,654	64	325	119	92	151

Source: Extract from COINS database, Administrative Court Office, January 2017

Notes:

1) For the more recent JR applications the figures are unlikely to be the final figures on case progressions, since cases need time to work their way through the Administrative Court system.

2) Includes Regional Offices of the Administrative Court, although most cases received were issued in London.

3) Timeliness figures only for applications granted, refused, or allowed or dismissed at final hearing. Including time spent "stood out" of the list.

4) The figures include cases that were transferred to the Upper Tribunal in the November 2013.

5) A small number of the Administrative Court Immigration and Asylum Judicial Reviews are transferred to the Upper Tribunal of the Immigration and Asylum Chamber (UTIAC) after a decision has been made in the process above. Where this has occurred they have been included in the timeliness figures above. However, the majority of cases transfer prior to reaching the permission stage.

APPENDIX E: Documents relating to my complaint against the deputy High Court judge.

a) My letter of complaint dated 8th June 2016.

Tel: ██████████(h)
████████████(m)

8th June 2016

The Judicial Conduct and Investigations Office,
81 – 82 Queens Building,
Royal Courts of Justice,
Strand,
London, WC2A 2LL.

Dear Sirs,

RE: R v ████████COUNTY COURT EX PARTE ████████████

In the above matter, by order dated the 14th April 2016, ████████, sitting as a Deputy High Court Judge, dismissed an application for permission to apply for judicial review and, ruling the application to be totally without merit, she ordered the matter should not be reconsidered at a hearing.

The essence of the judicial review application was accusations of serious misconduct and unfairness made against District Judge █████ (the trial judge) and, especially, Judge ████████(the appeal judge) in the conduct of a civil claim between ████████ & Co Ltd (Claimant) and Mr ████(Defendant). It is

1

with great regret that I now feel compelled to complain that **in making her order Ms. Justice██herself knowingly breached her oath of office by suppressing the application irrespective of its legal merits and by seeking to silence the accusations against the judges.** She did not act without fear or favour. Rather, she acted solely to protect her fellow judges and the image of the judiciary. Such behaviour amounts to misconduct in a public office albeit the judge enjoys the benefit of judicial immunity and cannot be prosecuted and thus this is not a matter for the police. Nonetheless, this is a complaint about conduct (even if the evidence rests in the judge's decision) and is not simply a complaint that the judge got the law wrong. Rather, it is a complaint that she never tried to get it right. She acted to defeat justice. She was dishonest. Her judgment was carefully crafted to ridicule the accusations and arguments being made.

Although the subject matter lying behind this complaint involves accusations of dishonesty against Judge ██████████ and District Judge ██████ this complaint is against Ms. Justice ██ alone.

The complaint details may be relatively complex and it may be necessary for the investigating judge to read the judicial review papers, yet this complaint is entirely within your remit as covered by The Judicial Discipline (Prescribed Procedures) Regulations 2014, where "complaint" is defined as "a complaint containing an allegation of misconduct by a person holding judicial office or other office", and within The Judicial Conduct (Judicial and other office holders) Rules 2014 which does not by virtue of rule 21 (b) exclude this complaint for although this complaint is about a judicial decision it **does** raise a question of misconduct. The rules envisage more onerous investigations than this complaint will require and this complaint is of serious misconduct.

My complaint must be clear and is necessarily worded strongly. That said, although I care greatly about the matter and I have no intention of letting it rest, I have tried to be matter of fact and, wherever possible, soften the tone and avoid the superlative.

2

In accordance with the rules you will find enclosed a copy of the claim for judicial review and supporting documentation together with the letter accompanying them dated the 15th October 2015, a letter from the appeal judge, Judge ████████ dated the 12th October 2015, forwarded to the Administrative Court under cover of letter dated the 11th November 2015 (copy also enclosed) just after the lodging of the judicial review for placing with the papers, and a copy of the judgment of Ms. Justice██.I have added by hand the Crown Office reference number to the Judicial Review Claim Form and the accompanying Index of Documents.

It is true that Mr███ could have applied to a judge of the Court of Appeal for permission for judicial review (rule 52.15 of the Civil Procedure Rules) but his not having done so does not in any way prohibit this complaint since it is irrelevant to the issue of misconduct on the part of Ms. Justice███. This is not an appeal. It is a complaint about misconduct. In any event, irrespective of any appeal, Mr ███ was entitled to a fair and honest determination of his application for permission by Ms. Justice███.

I am not saying that the judicial review was bound to succeed even though I believe, fairly and responsibly assessed, it ought to have succeeded. All of that is beside the point which is that the deliberation of Ms. Justice███ was not a fair process and her determination was the product of misconduct.

I know these accusations are extraordinary. I am a retired solicitor and I assisted Mr ███ throughout his case (I drafted all documents and I represented him at trial). I am the founder of Oslers Solicitors which continues to practice in Suffolk and Cambridgeshire. I stand by all I have represented in this case to date and I have no difficulty in demonstrating the dishonesty of Ms. Justice███. **The relevant standard of proof is the balance of probabilities** (rule 39 of The Judicial Conduct (Judicial and other office holders) Rules 2014).

Below are set out my arguments as to why it is clear that Ms. Justice███ acted dishonestly in this matter. If **any** part of her judgment shows her to have been dishonest then clearly this complaint must succeed and the whole of her judgment is tainted. Under the heading **"The Dishonesty of Ms. Justice███"** I

3

single out and deal solely with her view that the appeal judge could have made an order for costs due to unreasonable behaviour on the part of Mr ▆▆▆ (for ease of reference I shall refer to this as a wasted costs order although strictly speaking that term refers to an order against legal representatives) by looking at a record on the court file. That view is so erroneous it is not credible that a High Court judge acting honestly could advance it and it is the clearest evidence of Ms. Justice ▆▆'s mala fides. Under the heading **"Other Evidence of Ms. Justice ▆▆'s Dishonesty"** I deal with other aspects of her judgment which (should such be needed) put beyond doubt her dishonesty. Those aspects are the excessive use of the pejorative and the categorisation of "totally without merit", factual distortion and misrepresentation and errors of law.

THE DISHONESTY OF MS. JUSTICE ▆▆

Although the whole of Ms. Justice ▆▆'s decision is consistent with her having acted dishonestly, there is at least one part of it which is unarguably dishonest and that part is as follows:

"Any application for costs due to unreasonable behaviour may well have been recorded on file" (given by Ms. Justice ▆▆ as a possible justification for the appeal judge's decision to make a wasted costs order).

It is necessary to know the following facts regarding Mr ▆▆'s case:

1) On the original County Court Claim Form there was a claim for fixed costs of £80 being legal representative's costs (these assist in deterring frivolous defendants who unreasonably choose not to concede a claim early). However, these costs are not allowable if the case goes to trial (presumably in such a case a defendant is not seen as frivolous). At trial District Judge ▆▆ wrongly ordered Mr ▆▆ to pay the £80 fixed costs, a fact that has been accepted by the appeal judge and Ms. Justice ▆▆

4

2) A completely separate provision to that of fixed costs allows a judge in a small claim to override the usual "no costs" rule (see rule 27.14 of the Civil Procedure Rules) and to order costs against a party if they have behaved unreasonably. At trial an application for wasted costs was made against Mr ■■■ but District Judge ■■■ rejected it.

3) Following the trial an appeal was lodged and one of the grounds was that the order of the £80 fixed costs was an error by District Judge ■■■ (the trial judge). The Circuit Judge, Judge ■■■■■■(the appeal judge), clearly accepted that the trial judge had erred but dismissed the ground of appeal as having no real prospects of success saying "Pursuant to CPR r27.14, the District Judge may order one party to pay the Court fees, expenses, and further costs if that party has behaved unreasonably."

4) In the application for judicial review it was submitted that since court fees and expenses were not relevant to the appeal, and although Judge ■■■■■ had talked in the abstract ("the District Judge **may** order..."), it was clear she was in fact dismissing the ground of appeal relating to fixed costs by making a wasted costs order against Mr ■■■ in the sum of £80. It was further submitted that there was nothing in the Grounds of Appeal before Judge ■■■■■ as would have allowed her to make such an order. It was submitted that she had no legitimate reason to want to dismiss this ground of appeal, nor reason to think of making a wasted costs order, nor information as would permit a wasted costs order and that therefore she must have discussed the appeal with the trial judge who alone would want to advise the appeal judge of that possibility in light of the application made at the trial.

5

In the statement of Ms. Justice ▮ which I have highlighted above as being dishonest, she clearly accepts that there was nothing in the Grounds of Appeal as would have allowed Judge ▮▮▮▮▮ to make a wasted costs order. However, rejecting my argument that the appeal judge must have talked to the trial judge (which I will comment on later) she proffers the explanation that the appeal judge might have read a record on the court file of the wasted costs application made at the trial. **This attempt to find an explanation which bails out the appeal judge is demonstrably dishonest for the following reasons: firstly,** the notion that a wasted costs order could be made to replace an order for fixed costs on the Claim Form in a case in which there was a trial at which the defendant partly succeeded is so flawed as a matter of legal principle that it is not credible that a judge of the High Court acting honestly could believe otherwise; **secondly,** the procedure for the making of the wasted costs order by the appeal judge was so flawed that it is not credible that any judge of the High Court acting honestly would do anything but severely criticise it as manifestly unfair; **thirdly,** the appeal judge, when challenged, refused to explain and a High Court judge acting honestly would give significant weight to that; **fourthly,** Ms. Justice ▮ did not investigate as she could and should have done. In greater detail, I shall now take each of these four points in turn.

Making a wasted costs order in substitution for fixed costs on the Claim form

a) Ms. Justice ▮ clearly accepted that Judge ▮▮▮▮ made a wasted costs order against Mr ▮ in the sum of £80.

b) Since that order was to counter the ground of appeal dealing with the illegitimate fixed costs, the £80 in question must have been for those costs, namely the legal representative's costs on the Claim Form. These are costs for preparing the Claim Form.

6

c) A wasted costs order would be made without reference to the fixed costs provisions. They are completely separate and different provisions. It is fixed costs that are there to deal with any pre-claim frivolousness. Also, what a coincidence that in this case the wasted costs order happened to equal the fixed costs under appeal!

d) A wasted costs order for legal representative's costs would be calculated at an hourly rate on the basis of time spent. Such costs for preparing a Claim Form would far exceed £80.

e) Since they were on the Claim Form, the £80 costs would have to have been caused by behaviour **before** the Claim started. It is impossible that there would be pre-claim behaviour as would justify wasted costs in favour of a lawyer preparing a Claim Form in a case where the defendant went to trial and, in part, won. How could you unreasonably cause the preparation of a Claim Form in a case which you sincerely and legitimately defended to a trial at which you partly succeeded? Further, Mr███ was so sincere in his defence (which was not only legitimate but highly meritorious) that he lodged an appeal!

f) Had there been such pre-claim unreasonable behaviour then it is very difficult to see how its effect would not continue after the issue of the Claim Form. In other words it wouldn't have ended with the issue of the Claim. Such an order would likely run to hundreds if not thousands of pounds.

For the above reasons, the notion of making a wasted costs order to replace the order for the fixed legal representative's costs on the Claim Form is erroneous and it is not credible that a High Court judge would think otherwise.

7

The procedure for wasted costs and natural justice

a) The trial judge declined to make a wasted costs order after hearing representations. If Ms. Justice ██'s assertion that the appeal judge looked at the court file is right then the appeal judge would have known that fact. There was no appeal against this decision by ████████ & Co Ltd, the original Claimant, and it is oft said that a trial judge who has heard the evidence is best placed to decide facts and appeal judges should be slow to interfere with such findings. It is inconceivable that an appeal judge would overrule a trial judge based solely on an "application…..recorded on documents on file" (per Ms. Justice ██'s judgment).

b) The appeal judge should have specified in clear terms that she was making a wasted costs order. Rather, she used the abstract form ("may…") and included unnecessary reference to court fees and expenses.

c) The appeal judge had no reason to look on the court file for evidence in support of a wasted costs order. She should just have allowed the appeal to move forward on this ground. She should have approached her task without bias.

d) The appeal judge did not specify to the parties what unreasonable behaviour was of concern to her, furnishing them with a copy of any document relied on, and she did not give the parties an opportunity to make representations even though the trial judge had declined to make a wasted costs order. This was an astonishing breach of procedural fairness.

e) The appeal judge did not specify how she had calculated the sum of £80 and on what information she had relied in this regard.

8

183

f) Even still Mr ▮ has not received details of the supposed unreasonable behaviour and the evidence of it which led to the wasted costs order nor of how the sum was arrived at. It is clear Ms. Justice ▮ did not obtain the County Court file to check what was there but, rather, in addition to ignoring basic legal principles and procedural fairness, she has preferred to guess in favour of the appeal judge. It beggars belief.

For all the above reasons, the procedure accepted by Ms. Justice ▮ for the making of the wasted costs order by the appeal judge is a gross breach of the rules of natural justice and any High Court judge acting honestly would severely criticise it rather than advance it in defence of a Circuit Judge.

The appeal judge's refusal to explain

The appeal judge received a letter before action relating to the judicial review. That letter accused her of dishonestly making a wasted costs order and called upon her to explain if that accusation was wrong. Notwithstanding a judge's duty to give reasons for a decision, and notwithstanding the duty to respond to a letter before action, the appeal judge declined to comment. Any High Court judge acting honestly would give significant weight to this refusal to explain.

Ms. Justice ▮'s failure to investigate

Ms. Justice ▮ had before her accusations of a very serious nature made against two of Her Majesty's judges. It is clear she accepted that there was nothing in the Grounds of Appeal before Judge ▮ as would have justified a wasted costs order. The question therefore remained: why was a wasted costs order made? Ms. Justice ▮'s answer, in effect, is that she doesn't know! Isn't that extraordinary? Not only does Mr ▮ not know, not only does Judge ▮ refuse to explain, but even after complaint is made to a judge of the High Court, that judge does not know. Yet she is willing to categorise Mr ▮'s complaint as having no merit or substance.

9

All that Ms. Justice ⬛ does is to guess in favour of the appeal judge. But given the guess she made, why did she not follow it up and call for the County Court file? She could have ascertained for herself whether or not there was relevant material on that file. Had there not been, she would have known beyond any doubt that she had a dishonest Circuit Judge on her hands. It was an inexplicable failure on her part.

Even now, if the judiciary is serious about its integrity, it is not too late for someone to look at that court file. I know you will find nothing there (especially regarding pre-claim behaviour and information as would allow quantification of the costs) and it will be necessary to confront the fact of a dishonest Circuit Judge.

OTHER EVIDENCE OF MS. JUSTICE ⬛'S DISHONESTY

Although in light of the above it is not necessary to evidence further Ms. Justice ⬛'s dishonesty, there are so many other aspects of her judgment which support the accusation it would be remiss not to point them out. These fall into three categories: the excessive use of the pejorative and the categorisation of the claim as being "totally without merit", factual distortion and misrepresentation and errors of law. In greater detail, I shall now deal with each category.

The excessive use of the pejorative and the categorisation of "totally without merit"

Ms. Justice ⬛ found the application to be "totally without merit" the legal meaning of which is "bound to fail". In order to prevent the accusations against the appeal judge and the trial judge being made in open court (where others, including the press, might begin to take an interest), it was necessary for this finding to be made for it is only on this basis that an oral hearing for renewing the application for permission can be denied. But Ms. Justice ⬛ didn't stop there. Rather, she poured scorn on all my arguments using phrases such as "wholly unsatisfactory", "pure speculation", "quite simply no basis", "no hesitation in rejecting", "as for the underlying merits....there are none" and "nothing of substance in the remaining grounds". Taken as a whole, this evidences a judge who is at pains to emphasise how every aspect of the application is unmeritorious. She protests too much. It is a profoundly dishonest assessment and it lends credence to the view that the judge's decision was made to vehemently protect her fellow judges and the public image of the judiciary. The objective was to portray the application as ridiculous, to treat it with contempt, to kill it dead as forcefully as possible and to silence the accusations.

Factual distortion and misrepresentation

Dealing with Ms. Justice ██'s judgment in the order in which factual statements appear, the following observations can be made (paragraph references are to those in Ms. Justice ██'s judgment):

Paragraph 1

In so far as the judgment suggests that the explanation for the delay was based on only two things, namely, on the one hand, a slowness to see how unfair the appeal judge's decision was and, on the other hand, that the appeal judge had discussed the application with the trial judge (the latter being part of the explanation for the slowness), it is incomplete. The explanation for the delay was also based on a responsible hesitation before making serious accusations against judges and on an assertion that the appeal judge's decision was a deception. It is the reasons behind the being slow to understand that are surely all important.

Ms. Justice ██ states that the contention that the appeal judge and trial judge must have discussed the case is "pure speculation" and there is "quite simply no basis" for it. Yet she clearly accepts there was no basis in the Grounds of Appeal before the appeal judge for a wasted costs order. She proffers the infeasible possibility of reliance on a record on the court file (see earlier). It is known that the issue of wasted costs was raised at trial. There are only two possible explanations for the appeal judge's order and both are wholly improper: firstly, the appeal judge, without any personal motive, arbitrarily

11

decided the appeal was not going to go any further and, perhaps seeing mention of a wasted costs order on the court file, she thought she could use it as an excuse for her decision; or secondly, she did not arbitrarily dismiss the appeal but, rather, she discussed the case with the trial judge and drafted her judgment accordingly. The personal motive to assist a known colleague is more credible than an impersonal motive to arbitrarily defeat justice. Further, when the accusation of collusion was put to the appeal judge, she declined to comment notwithstanding her ongoing duty to give reasons for her decision and her duty to respond to the letter before action prior to the judicial review. All of this is far from "pure speculation". It is deductive reasoning and on the balance of probabilities the contention that the judges discussed the appeal is the most likely. Speculation is an essential part of our law – concepts such as "reasonable suspicion", "more likely than not" and "circumstantial but compelling" all demand a reasoned and informed speculation. However, even if there was no collusion, the alternative still means the appeal judge was dishonest and the appeal was an unfair process (of which there is absolutely no doubt).

Paragraph 2

Ms. Justice ▮ misrepresents the explanation given for not requesting an oral hearing. She implies the reason was that the appeal judge had reserved the matter to herself. In fact, the more important points were that the appeal judge had shown herself intent on dishonestly blocking the appeal and that she had unfairly imposed a condition precedent to the oral hearing, namely, the requirement for a transcript of the judgment given at trial.

Paragraph 3

Ms. Justice ▮ states that the challenge to the appeal judge's decision was "based on speculation that Judge ▮ had discussed the case with District Judge ▮". That is grossly misleading. The challenge was in part based on that contention but it was based also on the assertion that the appeal judge had blatantly ignored basic legal propositions which were well-supported by the facts and evidence; and on the bizarre wording of the appeal

12

judge's decision; and on the inexplicable order for a transcript of the trial judgment; and on the lack of any feasible reason for the making of the wasted costs order; and on the fact the appeal had been dismissed at the permission stage; and on the reference by the appeal judge to reliance on unspecified documentary evidence. All of which Ms. Justice⬛ found to have "nothing of substance".

Errors of law

This ought to read *apparent* errors of law for in truth they were not errors if they were deliberate. Further, these are additional to those set out under the heading "The Dishonesty of Ms. Justice⬛" above.

One of the accusations against the appeal judge was that she had deliberately ignored the law. Examples were given setting out basic legal propositions based on the evidence of the Claimant and supported by case law which the appeal judge had deemed to have "no real prospects of success". Since Ms. Justice⬛ considers this accusation to have "no merit" and "nothing of substance", she purports to think credible that a Circuit Judge could be honestly mistaken in finding that if B is going to occur whether or not A occurs nonetheless A can be a cause of B; and that if one suffers loss as a result of an error in a survey report one should not only be compensated for that loss but in addition one is entitled to reimbursement of the survey fee; and that notwithstanding a case report filed with the appeal papers clearly stating the measurement of loss for surveyor's negligence is diminution in value, nonetheless such an argument is without any merit! Ms. Justice⬛ cannot possibly believe that.

In paragraph 2 of her decision, Ms. Justice⬛ rules that Mr⬛ "failed to avail himself of the alternative remedy of requesting an oral hearing". She refers to the appeal judge having reserved the matter to herself as if that was the sole reason for not requesting an oral hearing but, as set out in the previous section, that is a misrepresentation of the facts. In any event, the following observations can be made:

13

i)	The accusations against the appeal judge were that she had deliberately denied the appeal notwithstanding its overwhelming merits. She was biased. She breached her oath of office. She ignored the law. She conspired with the trial judge. Further, it was alleged that, as part of her unfair dealing with the appeal, she unfairly imposed an impediment to the request for an oral hearing, namely, an order that a transcript of the judgment given at trial be obtained. This was a condition precedent to the oral hearing. It is true that she also reserved the oral hearing to herself. If those accusations were true then no sensible person is going to hold that a failure to request an oral hearing should prejudice a later complaint by way of judicial review. The oral hearing would have been a "kangaroo court" and the condition precedent an unfair deterrent. Thus, the issue of the oral hearing as an alternative remedy becomes a red-herring and the real issue is did the appeal judge act as alleged.

ii)	To appear before the same judge and say the same things that she has already unequivocally ruled on is hardly a remedy.

iii)	It is well-established that each stage in court proceedings should be a fair process. The fact there is a subsequent stage does not cure any unfairness in a previous one. Parliament intended that Mr■■■ should have had a fair application for permission at the paper stage and that he should have had a fair oral hearing thereafter. That his paper application was an unfair process is not cured by the offer of an oral hearing. The only remedy available to cure the unfairness of the paper application was judicial review

14

iv)   The fact which prompted Mr ███ to make his
        complaint was that the trial judge and the appeal judge
        had colluded to defeat the appeal. At the time of his
        realising that fact the time for requesting an oral
        hearing before the appeal judge had long passed and it
        would not have been realistic to seek an extension of
        time. The only available remedy was judicial review.
        There was no alternative.

Again, the stated views of Ms. Justice ███ encompassed by her decision are
inconsistent with a High Court judge acting honestly.

The judicial review was an opportunity for the High Court to show its maturity
and honour. Ms. Justice ███ failed to do so. It is not too late. Show us, please,
that the boasts of our senior judges as to the Rule of Law, the Magna Carta, the
integrity of our judges and the rights of the individual are, in the final analysis,
true.

I am willing to meet to discuss this complaint and its resolution at any time.

                    Yours faithfully,

                    Paul Osler

                        15

b) Rule 21(b) of The Judicial Conduct (Judicial and other office holders) Rules 2014 (contains public sector information licensed under the Open Government Licence v3.0.).

permitted address.	address on a business day before 4.30pm, that day; or in any case, if delivered at, or after, 4.30pm, the next business day.
Fax.	If the transmission of the fax is completed on a business day before 4.30pm, that day; or in any other case, if transmitted at, or after, 4.30pm, the next business day.
Other electronic method.	If an e-mail or other electronic transmission is sent on a business day before 4.30pm, that day; or in any other case, if an e-mail or other electronic transmission is sent at, or after, 4.30pm, the next business day.

PART 2

Investigation by the Judicial Conduct Investigations Office

Scope

19. This Part applies where—

(a) a complaint is made to the Judicial Conduct Investigations Office;

(b) the Lord Chancellor and the Lord Chief Justice refer a complaint to the Judicial Conduct Investigations Office in accordance with regulation 13 of the Regulations;

(c) the Ombudsman refers a case to the Judicial Conduct Investigations Office to investigate under section 111(7)(b) of the Act; or

(d) a nominated judge refers a case to the Judicial Conduct Investigations Office under rule 97.

The investigation process by the Judicial Conduct Investigations Office

20. A complaint must initially be considered by the Judicial Conduct Investigations Office.

21. The Judicial Conduct Investigations Office must dismiss a complaint, or part of a complaint, if it falls into any of the following categories—

(a) it does not adequately particularise the matter complained of;

(b) it is about a judicial decision or judicial case management, and raises no question of misconduct;

(c) the action complained of was not done or caused to be done by a person holding an office;

(d) it is vexatious;

(e) it is without substance;

(f) even if true, it would not require any disciplinary action to be taken;

(g) it is untrue, mistaken or misconceived;

(h) it raises a matter which has already been dealt with, whether under these Rules or otherwise, and does not present any material new evidence;

(i) it is about a person who no longer holds an office;

(j) it is about the private life of a person holding an office and could not reasonably be considered to affect their suitability to hold office;

191

c) Letter dated 28th June 2016 from the JCIO, rejecting my complaint.

Judicial Conduct
Investigations Office

Judicial Conduct Investigations
Office
81 & 82 Queens Building
Royal Courts of Justice
Strand
London
WC2A 2LL
DX44450 Strand

T 020 7 073 4805

http://judicialconduct.judiciary.gov.uk

Mr Osler

Our ref: ████/2016

28 June 2016

Dear Mr Osler

Your complaint about Ms Justice ██

I am writing further to your complaint dated 8 June 2016 to inform you that the Judicial Conduct Investigations Office (JCIO) is unable to accept your complaint for consideration. This is because your complaint does not contain an allegation of misconduct on the part of a named judicial office holder. Rule 8 of the Judicial Conduct (Judicial and other office holders) Rules 2014 requires that your complaint meets this criterion if it is to be considered as valid. Details of these Rules can be found on our website, the address of which is detailed above.

The independence of the judiciary means that judges must be free to make decisions without interference from government officials or even other judges unless they are presiding over the case. For this reason the JCIO cannot comment on the decisions or case management of judges. Such decisions include, but are not restricted to: a Judge's decision on whether a case raises a personal conflict of interest, decisions taken on the management of a case as it progresses; matters relating to the judgment, sentencing and other ancillary decisions such as costs. Nor can we consider complaints about the weight that Judges have given to evidence, the accuracy of their assessment of witnesses, or the decisions they have made. There are no circumstances in which we can seek to challenge, investigate, vary or overturn the decisions which a Judge has made in the course of a hearing. Whether those decisions were correct or incorrect is not a matter for this office. The only way in which such decisions may be challenged is by appeal to a higher court.

Having considered the matters you have raised, your complaint refers to Ms Justice ██'s management and decisions in the case and raises no suggestion of judicial misconduct. An important part of the judicial function is to weigh up evidence and decide on its relevance in determining how to proceed with a case or making a judgment. The fact that you disagree with the decisions made in the case and the evidence relied upon in arriving at those decisions does not make it a matter of misconduct. It was for Ms Justice ██ to decide upon the evidence to be heard in the matter, and the weight to be placed upon the aforesaid. Whilst you are of the view that the Judge was dishonest in her decision making and acted to defeat justice, this office cannot consider a judge's competence, diligence or whether the decisions made were correct in law. Similarly, it is not for this office to determine whether, for whatever reason, a judge has correctly managed a case.

In essence, it is for a judge to determine how they want a case to run, who can speak at what point, what evidence to take into consideration and from whom. It is also for a Judge to determine what actions need to be taken in order to progress a matter and to decide upon whether to strike out an application or not, the judgment to be handed down, and Orders, Rulings and Directions made.

It is for this reason that I am unable to take your complaint forward.

The appropriate way to challenge a Judge's decision is through the appeal process, although it is not guaranteed that there would be a right of appeal. Alternatively, you may be able to challenge the decision by judicial review. As members of staff at the JCIO are not legally trained we suggest that you may wish to consider seeking legal advice in order to find out what your options are in relation to an appeal and how to proceed.

You may find it helpful to seek advice from a solicitor, law centre or the Citizen's Advice Bureau (http://www.citizensadvice.org.uk). The Civil Legal Service (CLS) – a Government organisation – might also be able to help. This service helps put people in touch with sources of legal advice in their area. Further details about the CLS can be found on their website (https://www.gov.uk/civil-legal-advice).

The Bar Pro Bono Unit may also be of assistance. The Unit receives applications for assistance through advice agencies and solicitors. The Unit aims to help in cases where the applicant cannot afford to pay for the assistance sought or obtain public funding, has a meritorious case, and needs the help a barrister can provide. Further details about the charity and how to apply can be found on their website: www.barprobono.org.uk

Judicial Appointments and Conduct Ombudsman

If you are unhappy about my handling of your complaint, you should contact the Judicial Appointments and Conduct Ombudsman. The Ombudsman can consider complaints about how I have handled your complaint, but he does not have the power to investigate your original complaint to the JCIO.

The Ombudsman will consider a complaint if you write to him within 28 days of our decision. After this time, he will consider whether he is able to investigate it. You can contact the Ombudsman:

- in writing at: *9th Floor Tower, 9.53, 102 Petty France, London, SW1H 9AJ*;

- by e-mail at headofoffice@jaco.gsi.gov.uk; and

- by telephone on 020 3334 2900.

For further information about the Ombudsman see www.judicialombudsman.gov.uk.

d) Extract from the JCIO's Supplementary Guidance on the rules, giving their definition of "misconduct" (see under "Rule 6") and their interpretation of Rule 21(b) (contains public sector information licensed under the Open Government Licence v3.0.).

The JACO cannot comment on the merits of any decision made in respect of a particular case however if satisfied that the grounds of the complaint to him are justified he may make recommendations to the Lord Chancellor and the Lord Chief Justice. If the JACO considers any decision to be unreliable as a result of maladministration he can set the decision aside and refer the matter back to the JCIO to be started afresh.

A complaint to JACO should be made within 28 days of receipt of the final letter indicating the outcome of your complaint. Further information about the Ombudsman's role can be found at www.justice.gov.uk/about/jaco/how-to-make-a-complaint or by telephoning: 0203 334 2900.

9.Confidentiality

Section 139 of the Constitutional Reform Act 2005

Section 139 of the Constitutional Reform Act (CRA)prohibits someone who obtains or is given confidential information for the purposes of dealing with judicial complaints and discipline disclosing it except with lawful authority. The information is confidential if it relates to an identified or identifiable individual. It can only be lawfully disclosed if one of the following conditions is met:

(a) each person to whom the information relates (this includes the giver of an opinion about another, as well as the person referred to) agrees;

(b) the disclosure is for, and is necessary for the exercise of functions under the discipline provisions of the Act, or of section 11(3A) of the Supreme Court Act; or the regulations and rules made under the Constitutional Reform Act; or

(c) disclosure is required under rules of court or a court order for the purposes
of legal proceedings.

Information about disciplinary action can, however, be disclosed if the Lord Chancellor and the Lord Chief Justice so agree. The section does not prevent the disclosure of information which is already, or has previously been, available to the public from other sources.

Information provided during the course of a complaint or conduct investigation should be considered to be confidential to the person who disclosed it (whether the complainant, the subject of the complaint or a third party) but may be disclosed in accordance with S139 of the CRA 2005 and should be treated as such. Any queries in relation to specific cases should be addressed to the JCIO.

[Please Note: reference should be made to the full text of section 139 of the Constitutional Reform Act 2005 for the full details of requirements in relation to confidentiality]

10. Guidance to the Rules

Rule 6: The JCIO may only consider a complaint that contains an allegation of misconduct by a judge or other office holder. Such misconduct relates to the judge's personal behaviour for example: a judge shouting or speaking in a sarcastic manner in court; or misuse of judicial status outside of court. It does not relate to decisions or judgments made by a judge in the course of court proceedings. The only way to challenge such matters is through the appellate process.

194

Where a complaint does not contain an allegation of misconduct the JCIO will advise the complainant that it cannot investigate the complaint and will inform the complainant of the reasons for rejection.

Complaints made by HMCTS/ MoJ staff or judicial office holders

It is expected that the appropriate internal grievance process will have been fully considered as a possible means of dealing with a complaint when the matter relates to complaints made by HMCTS /MoJ staff , or are made by a judicial office holder about a fellow judicial office holder. The Judicial HR within the Judicial Office is able to provide advice and support in respect of the internal grievance process.

Rule 7: Complaints must be made to the JCIO in writing however special arrangements may be made for anyone who is unable to write down a complaint, for example because of language difficulties or disability.

Rule 10: Unless there is evidence to suggest otherwise, it is assumed that the submission of a complaint implies consent to disclose it and the name of the complainant to the subject of the complaint and anyone who may be able to assist with the investigation of the complaint. Complaints will not be accepted by the Judicial Complaints Investigations Office where the complainant states that they do not want their identity disclosed to the subject of the disciplinary proceedings.

Rule 14: Representations requesting to extend the time limit for accepting a complaint must be made in writing to the JCIO, and must set out clearly the reasons why it was not possible to lodge the complaint with the JCIO within three months of the alleged misconduct.

Rule 15: The JCIO may only extend the time limit where it is satisfied that there are exceptional reasons as to why the complainant was unable to lodge the complaint within three months of the matter complained of.

Rule 21 (a) A complaint must set out all the details required under rule 5 and provide specific details about the alleged misconduct. For example a complaint which simply states that a judge was rude is not adequately particularised. In this example the complainant should state what the judge said or did to cause the complainant to believe that the judge was behaving inappropriately and at which part of the hearing this occurred.

Rule 21(b) The constitutional independence of the judiciary means that decisions made by a judicial office holder during the course of proceedings are made without the interference of ministers, officials or other judicial office holders (unless they are considering the matter whilst sitting in their judicial capacity, for example, in an appeal hearing). Judicial decisions include, but are not limited to, the way in which proceedings are managed, disclosure of documents, what evidence should be heard and the judgment or sentence given.

Rule 21 (d): In many cases vexation is inferred from a pattern of past complaints and the absence of reasonable cause.

Rule 21 (e): A complaint may be dismissed under this rule in circumstances where a complaint is adequately particularised but it bears no relationship to real facts.

e) My referral to the ombudsman, setting out in box 4 my arguments for him to carry out a review.

The JCIO has refused to consider my complaint on the ground that it does not contain an allegation of misconduct. Actually, my complaint alleges serious misconduct against the judge. It couldn't be clearer.

In their letter they state "There are no circumstances in which we can seek to challenge, investigate, vary or overturn the decisions which a judge has made in the course of a hearing". Why then does Rule 21(b) of the Judicial Conduct (Judicial and other office holders) Rules 2014 permit a complaint "about a judicial decision" where a question of misconduct is raised? It follows that there must be circumstances in which the JCIO has to investigate a judge's decision.They say "Whilst you are of the view that the judge was dishonest in her decision making and acted to defeat justice, this office cannot consider a judge's competence, diligence or whether the decisions made were correct in law". Acting dishonestly and to defeat justice would clearly be misconduct and it is a very different question to that of a judge's " competence, diligence...". I have not complained that the judge was incompetent or simply wrong. I have complained that she deliberately suppressed the appeal, breached her oath of office, was dishonest and acted to defeat justice and to protect her fellow judges and the image of the judiciary i.e I have alleged serious misconduct.

The JCIO is following the published "Supplementary Guidance" to the above rules which at paragraph 10 deals with both Rule 6 and Rule 21(b). Regulation 4(4) of the Judicial Discipline (Prescribed Procedures) Regulations 2014 allows the JCIO to provide advice on the application and interpretation of the rules and regulations but the Guidance cannot change, add to, subtract from or overrule the Rules which have statutory authority. The Guidance contradicts the Rules and the Rules take precedence. Under "Rule 6" the Guidance says "misconduct relates to the judge's personal behaviour...It does not relate to decisions or judgements made by a judge in the course of court proceedings". That cannot be right in so far as it seeks to exclude a judge's improper motives as misconduct for if it were so one would never complain about a judge's decision yet Rule 21(b) clearly permits such. Further, nowhere in the statutory regulations or rules is "misconduct" defined let alone limited to a judge's "personal behaviour". It is an ordinary word of the English language and needs no interpretation. Under "Rule 21 (b)" the Guidance says "The constitutional independence of the judiciary means that decisions made by a judicial office holder during the course of proceedings are made without interference of ministers, officials or other judicial office holders..". Here the Guidance seems again to want to say that the JCIO cannot investigate a judicial decision and yet Rule 21(b) clearly means one can complain "about" a judicial decision where an issue of misconduct is raised. My complaint is about a judicial decision and it raises an issue of misconduct. It is a valid complaint within the statutory rules and I want it processed accordingly.

I want the JCIO to be told that my complaint is about a judicial decision and raises an issue of misconduct as envisaged by Rule 21(b) and that they should deal with it in accordance with Rule 25 of the Judicial Conduct (Judicial and other office holders) Rues 2014.

f) Letter dated 22nd July 2016 from the ombudsman,
   accompanying his decision on my referral.

Judicial Appointments & Conduct Ombudsman
Postal Area 9.53
9th Floor, The Tower
102 Petty France
London
SW1H 9AJ
DX 152380 Westminster 8

T 020 3334 2900
E headofoffice@jaco.gsi.gov.uk

www.judicialombudsman.gov.uk

PRIVATE AND CONFIDENTIAL
Mr P A Osler

22 July 2016   Your ref: ▆▆▆▆▆

Dear Mr Osler

Your complaint

Thank you for your correspondence with my officers setting out your concerns
about the Judicial Conduct Investigations Office's handling of your complaint
about Ms Justice▆▆▆.

I have now completed a preliminary investigation into your complaint and I
enclose a copy of my report. I do not believe a review is necessary as there is
no prospect of any finding of maladministration.

I realise that this will be a disappointment to you, but would like to assure you that I
considered both the handling of your complaint and the points that you raised most
carefully.

Yours sincerely,

Mr Paul Kernaghan CBE, QPM

g) The ombudsman's decision and report dated 22nd July 2016.

Complaint by Mr Paul Osler
Ombudsman's Investigation Report

JUDICIAL APPOINTMENTS AND CONDUCT OMBUDSMAN'S REPORT

COMPLAINT BY MR PAUL OSLER

Introduction

Mr Osler wrote to me on 4 July 2016 and asked me to review the investigation carried out by the Judicial Conduct Investigations Office (JCIO) in relation to the complaint he had raised about Ms Justice ███.

My remit

In accordance with Section 110(2) of the Constitutional Reform Act 2005, I am required to review a complaint where 3 conditions have been met, the first of which is that I consider a review to be necessary. My remit specifically precludes me from reviewing decisions taken by those considering conduct complaints; I can look only at the process by which those complaints were handled. I enclose a copy of the relevant part of the Constitutional Reform Act 2005.

Mr Osler's complaint to me

Mr Osler complained, among other issues, that –

- In their letter, the JCIO state "There are no circumstances in which we can seek to challenge, investigate, vary or overturn the decisions which a judge had made in the course of a hearing". Why then does Rule 21(b) of the Judicial Conduct (Judicial and other office holders) Rules 2014 permit a complaint "about a judicial decision" where a question of misconduct is raised? It follows that there must be circumstances in which the JCIO has to investigate a judge's decision.

- The JCIO is following the published "Supplementary Guidance" to the rules, which at paragraph 10, deals with both Rule 6 and Rule 21(b). Regulation 4(4) of the Judicial Discipline (Prescribed Procedures) Regulations 2014 allows the JCIO to provide advice on the application and interpretation of the rules and regulations, but the Guidance cannot change, add to, subtract from or overrule the Rules, which have statutory authority. The Guidance contradicts the rules and regulations, but the Guidance says "misconduct relates to the judge's personal behaviour…it does not relate to decisions or judgments made by a judge in the course of court proceedings". That cannot be right, insofar as it seeks to exclude a judge's improper motives as misconduct, for if it were so, one would never complain about a judge's decision, yet Rule 21(b) clearly permits such.

- His complaint is about a judicial decision and it raises an issue of misconduct. It is a valid complaint within the statutory rules and should be processed accordingly.

My decision

I have decided that Mr Osler's complaint does not warrant a full investigation. In reaching this conclusion, I am commenting solely on the process by which the JCIO considered the complaint under the arrangements for dealing with concerns about judicial office holders' personal conduct. I cannot comment on the merits of the JCIO's decision or his case before Ms Justice ▇▇.

Factors taken into account

I have taken the following factors into account in reaching my decision:

- Mr Osler's views, as expressed in his correspondence with my office and previously with the JCIO; and
- The JCIO's papers regarding the handling of the complaint.

Mr Osler's complaint to the JCIO

Mr Osler wrote to the JCIO on 8 June 2016 and explained that, by Order dated 14 April 2016, Ms Justice ▇▇ dismissed an application for permission to apply for judicial review and, ruling the application to be totally without merit, ordered the matter should not be reconsidered at a hearing. Mr Osler complained, among other issues, that –

- In making her Order, Ms Justice ▇▇ knowingly breached her oath of office by suppressing the application, irrespective of its legal merits, and by seeking to silence the accusations made against other judges. She did not act without fear or favour. Rather, she acted solely to protect her fellow judges and the image of the judiciary. Such behaviour amounts to misconduct in a public office.

- This is a complaint about conduct (even if the evidence rests in the judge's decision) and it is not simply a complaint that the judge got the law wrong. Rather, it is a complaint that she never tried to get it right.

- The judge acted to defeat justice. She was dishonest and her judgment was carefully crafted to ridicule the accusations and arguments being made.

- The deliberation of Ms Justice ▇▇ was not a fair process and her determination was the product of misconduct.

- Aspects of Ms Justice ▇▇'s judgment put beyond doubt her dishonesty. Those aspects are the excessive use of the pejorative and the categorisation of "totally without merit", factual distortion and misrepresentation, and errors of law.

- Although the whole of Ms Justice ▇▇'s decision is consistent with her having acted dishonestly, there is at least one part of it which is unarguably dishonest and that part is – "Any application for costs due to unreasonable

199

behaviour may well have been recorded on file" (given by Ms Justice ▇▇ as a possible justification for the appeal judge's decision to make a wasted costs order).

The JCIO wrote to Mr Osler on 28 June 2016 and explained that they were unable to accept his complaint for consideration because it did not contain an allegation of misconduct on the part of a judicial office holder. They also explained that Rule 8 of the Judicial Conduct (Judicial and other office holders) Rules 2014 required that the complaint meet this criterion if it was to be considered as valid.

The JCIO explained that there were no circumstances in which they could seek to challenge, investigate, vary or overturn the decisions a judge has made in the course of a hearing. Whether those decisions were correct or incorrect was not a matter for them and the only way in which such decisions could be challenged was by appeal to a higher Court. Having considered the matters raised, the JCIO advised Mr Osler that his complaint referred to Ms Justice ▇▇'s management and decisions in the case and raised no suggestion of judicial misconduct.

The JCIO explained that, an important part of the judicial function was to weigh up evidence and decide on its relevance in determining how to proceed with a case or making a judgment. The fact that Mr Osler disagreed with the decisions made in the case and the evidence relied upon in arriving at those decisions, did not make it a matter of misconduct. It was for Ms Justice ▇▇ to decide upon the evidence to be heard in the matter and the weight to be placed upon it.

The JCIO stated that, whilst Mr Osler was of the view that the judge was dishonest in her decision making and acted to defeat justice, they could not consider a judge's competence, diligence or whether the decisions made were correct in law. Similarly, it was not for the JCIO to determine whether, for whatever reason, a judge had correctly managed a case. Therefore, the complaint could not be taken forward and Mr Osler was advised that he could write to my office if unhappy with the handling of his complaint.

My findings

I have considered the points Mr Osler raised in order to determine whether his complaint falls within my remit to investigate and my view is that the JCIO handled Mr Osler's complaint properly and correctly and the decision was consistent with the legislation as set in the Judicial Conduct (Judicial and other office holders) Rules 2014 and the appropriate guidance.

- The JCIO's view that the issues raised by Mr Osler related to Ms Justice ▇▇'s judicial decision-making and case management and not his personal conduct was consistent with its guidance. Leaflet JCIO1 on the JCIO website states that:

> "A Judge's role in court is to make independent decisions about cases and their management. These are often tough decisions, and Judges have to be firm and direct in the management of their cases. Examples of Judges' decisions include the length or type of sentence, whether a claim can proceed to trial, whether or not a claimant succeeds in their claim, what costs should be awarded and what evidence should be heard."

"This sort of decision cannot form the subject of a complaint. If you are unhappy with such a decision you are advised to seek legal advice from a solicitor, local law centre, Citizens Advice Bureau or the Community Legal Service to discuss whether you have a right of appeal."

"If your complaint is not about a Judge's decision but about the Judge's personal conduct you have the right to complain to the JCIO. Examples of potential personal misconduct would be the use of insulting, racist or sexist language".

- The JCIO clearly explained why Ms Justice ███'s decisions did not relate to his judicial conduct and appropriately advised Mr Osler that these concerns could only be addressed via the appeal process.

- I can see no substance in Mr Osler's claim that the JCIO failed to carry out the appropriate investigations into his complaint, in accordance with the Judicial Conduct (Judicial and other office holders) Rules 2014. They properly advised Mr Osler that his complaint did not contain an allegation of misconduct on the part of a named judicial office holder and so, did not meet the criteria set out under Rule 8 of the complaint rules for his complaint to be considered valid. This decision was made following an initial evaluation of the complaints raised by Mr Osler and I can see no issue with the JCIO's handling his complaint.

- Mr Osler correctly points out that Rule 21(b) of the Judicial Conduct (Judicial and other office holders) rules 2014 only enables the JCIO to dismiss complaints if they are about judicial decisions or judicial case management, and they do not raise a question of misconduct. This indicates that complaints about judicial decisions and judicial case management can be considered if there was evidence of misconduct in the decision. However, Mr Osler has provided no evidence that this occurred in this case, therefore, there was no requirement for the JCIO to investigate his complaint further.

I do not believe that Mr Osler has provided me with any examples of maladministration in respect of how the JCIO failed to investigate his complaint properly and, in accordance with Section 110(3) of the Constitutional Reform Act 2005, I do not consider that a review is necessary.

Mr Paul Kernaghan CBE, QPM

22 July 2016

h) My email dated 16th August 2016, requesting further explanation from the JCIO.

Complaint Ref█████2016

From: **paul osler**████████████
Sent: 16 August 2016 08:42:31
To: inbox@jcio.gsi.gov.uk (inbox@jcio.gsi.gov.uk)

Dear Sirs,

as you know, I referred your rejection of my above complaint to the Ombudsman and he ruled in your favour. I continue to disagree with your position (and that of the Ombudsman) but in seeking to understand it better I have the following questions which you might assist me with:

1) You have applied your own Supplementary Guidance. Can you confirm that the Guidance was issued in exercise of the power set out in Regulation 4(4) of the Judicial Discipline (Prescribed Procedures) Regulations 2014, namely the power to advise on the application and interpretation of the Rules and Regulations?

2) The Guidance defines "misconduct" as "personal misconduct" the latter being a definition which is not found in the Rules or Regulations. Is there any legal authority which says "misconduct" means "personal misconduct" or do you say your power to advise on the application and interpretation of the Rules and Regulations gives you authority to apply that definition?

3) Is there any legal authority that your power to advise on the application and interpretation of the Rules and Regulations allows you to define or expand on the meaning of words and phrases in the Rules and Regulations?

4) Who drafted and authorised the Supplementary Guidance?

Subject to your answers to the above questions, I would like to place this matter before the Administrative Court in an application for judicial review. Since you are not partisan on the issue and have no vested interest in the outcome (your interest presumably being merely that the correct legal position be stated), I suspect you would not participate in the judicial review but rather you would simply leave it up to the judge who will have your arguments as set out in your letter dated the 28th June, the Supplementary Guidance and the Ombudsman's decision. If you were to participate, I suspect you would not be inclined to instruct lawyers with the expense that such would involve. If I am right that you would not participate or would not instruct lawyers then it would seem only fair that for my part too I should not instruct lawyers as then you would not be at risk of my lawyers' fees if I won (the only costs in play would be court fees and out-of-pocket expenses). Am I right in thinking that you would not actively participate in the judicial review or, if you were to participate, you would not instruct lawyers?

Because of the time limit for judicial review (the long-stop of 3 months in this matter expires on the 28th September but, as you know, there is a duty to move to judicial review as soon as possible and without unreasonable delay) I would greatly appreciate a prompt reply which from what I have seen is your practice in any event.

I thank you for your ongoing assistance with this matter.

Paul Osler

i) Letter dated 9th September 2016 from the JCIO, clarifying its reasoning.

Judicial Conduct
Investigations Office

Judicial Conduct Investigations
Office
81 & 82 Queens Building
Royal Courts of Justice
Strand
London
WC2A 2LL
DX44450 Strand

T 020 7073 4719
E inbox@jcio.gsi.gov.uk

http://judicialconduct.judiciary.gov.uk

Mr Paul Osler
By email: ███████████████

Case number: ████ /2016

9 September 2016

Dear Mr Osler

Letter of Proposed Claim for Judicial Review

Thank you for your email of 15 August 2016. I am sorry for the delay in providing you with a substantive response. We are currently experiencing staff shortages that are impacting on the time taken to respond to correspondence in relation to closed cases. We are treating your email as a letter before claim and would be obliged if you would take this letter as our response under the pre-action protocol for judicial review.

In response to your specific questions:

1. I confirm that Regulation 4(4) of the Judicial Discipline (Prescribed Procedures) Rules 2014 states that the JCIO may provide advice to any person regarding the application and interpretation of the Regulations and any rules made under the Regulations. Any supplementary guidance issued is done so in accordance with the provisions of Regulation 4(4).

2. The Judicial Conduct (Judicial and other office holders) Rules 2014 specify the circumstances under which the JCIO must dismiss a complaint (see rule 21(a) to (l)). This includes complaints about judicial decision and case management, which do not constitute matters of misconduct. Therefore, any complaint relating to matters of judicial decision and case management only fall to be rejected as not containing an allegation of misconduct. As misconduct cannot include matters of judicial decision and case management, because these are matters of judicial function, misconduct must be personal on the part of the office holder.

3. The legal authority for the JCIO's role within the discipline process is as set out in Regulation 4.

4. The supplementary guidance on the conduct rules was drafted and approved by Mrs Judith Anckorn, at the time Head of the JCIO.

1. The Claimant

Mr Paul Osler

2. From

The Judicial Conduct Investigations Office (JCIO)

81 & 82 Queens Building

Royal Courts of Justice

Strand

London

WC2A 2LL

3. Reference Details

██████2016. Caseworker ████████████

4. The detail of the matter being challenged

You sent complaint form to the JCIO on 8 June 2016 about the conduct of Mr Justice██ in relation to the case of R v ███████County Court Ex Parte ████████ You complained about the decision made by Mrs Justice ██ in refusing your application for permission to apply for judicial review.

On considering the information you provided in your complaint, the caseworker explained that the Judicial Conduct Investigations Office (JCIO) was rejecting your complaint in accordance with Rule 8 of the Judicial Conduct (Judicial and other office holders) 2014 as your complaint related to Mrs Justice██s decision and case management and therefore did not contain an allegation of misconduct.

5. Response to Proposed Claim

The JCIO contests any claim in full. The JCIO determines complaints in accordance with the Judicial Conduct (Judicial and other office holders) Rules 2014. Your complaint was rejected in accordance with Rule 8 of these Rules.

The JCIO is satisfied that this decision was correct and made in accordance with the provisions of the Rules. The Judicial Appointments and Conduct Ombudsman has reviewed the JCIO's handling of your complaint and has not upheld your complaint to them.

6. Details of any other interested parties

None.

7. Address for further correspondence and service of court documents

If you wish to respond to this letter you may write to Mrs Clare Farren JCIO, 81&82 Queens Building, Royal Courts of Justice, Strand, London, WC2A 2LL. If you wish to serve court documents, you may serve them on the Treasury Solicitor's Department, One Kemble Street, London WC2B 4TS.

Yours sincerely,

j) My email dated 12th September 2016 to the ombudsman, asking him to revisit his decision.

Complaint of Paul Osler

paul osler

Mon 12/09/2016 13:51

To: headofoffice@jaco.gsi.gov.uk <headofoffice@jaco.gsi.gov.uk>;

 @jcio.gsi.gov.uk ████ @jcio.gsi.gov.uk>;

📎 1 attachments (56 KB)
Letter to Mr Osler 9 Sept 16 ████.doc;

My above complaint related to a decision of the JCIO to treat a complaint made to them against Deputy High Court Judge ██ as being invalid. In a decision dated the 22nd July, Mr Kernaghan ruled in favour of the JCIO.

Subsequent to Mr Kernaghan's decision and in contemplation of a judicial review, I wrote to the JCIO asking if they could either refer me to any legal authority to the effect that "misconduct" means "personal misconduct" or confirm that they were so defining it in exercise of powers given to them to issue guidance on interpretation. Their answer is such that, had it been known to Mr Kernaghan, it would surely have led to him finding against the JCIO. We are all under an obligation to reconsider our views so that unnecessary judicial reviews can be avoided and I wonder would Mr Kernaghan be prepared to revisit his decision?

The JCIO's answer to my question is that the rules are such that **ANY** complaint about a judicial decision is prohibited and "As misconduct cannot include matters of judicial decision and case management, because these are matters of judicial function, misconduct must be personal on the part of the office holder". In other words, their logic for defining "misconduct" as "personal misconduct" is founded on the notion that one can never complain about a judicial decision. Mr Kernaghan accepted that notion was incorrect and, seeing that it has erroneously led to the JCIO treating "misconduct" as "personal misconduct", he would surely now hold that to be an error - the very foundation of the JCIO's reasoning is something Mr Kernaghan found to be wrong!

I attach a copy of the letter from the JCIO dated the 9th September (see page 1 point 2)

Regards,

Paul Osler

k) Letter dated 26th September 2016 from the ombudsman,
again rejecting my complaint.

**Judicial Appointments & Conduct
Ombudsman**
Postal Area 9.53
9th Floor, The Tower
102 Petty France
London
SW1H 9AJ
DX 152380 Westminster 8

PRIVATE AND CONFIDENTIAL
Mr P A Osler

T 020 3334 2900
E headofoffice@jaco.gsi.gov.uk

www.judicialombudsman.gov.uk

26 September 2016

Your ref:

Dear Mr Osler

Your complaint

Thank you for your email, dated 12 September 2016, with attached response
to your proposed claim for Judicial Review, dated 9 September 2016, from the
Judicial Conduct Investigations Office (JCIO). I note the points you raise and
your request that I revisit my decision on your complaint, as set out in my
report to you, dated 22 July 2016.

My remit was to consider the process by which the JCIO handled your
complaint about Ms Justice ⬛ I cannot comment on or review the decisions
made by the JCIO during their investigation. Having reconsidered the
correspondence on this complaint, it is my view that the JCIO' assessment that
your concerns related to judicial decisions or case management was
consistent with guidance. The JCIO could not review the merits of Ms Justice
⬛'s decisions and there was no evidence of misconduct that the JCIO could
consider. In addition, the JCIO clearly explained why the judicial decisions
made by Ms Justice ⬛ in the course of your case did not relate to judicial
misconduct.

Therefore, there was no requirement for the JCIO to investigate your complaint
further and there was no evidence of maladministration in the JCIO's
investigation process. I understand your disappointment that your complaint
has not been resolved as you would wish, but I must now bring our
correspondence to a close.

APPENDIX F: Correspondence with the MPs.

a) My email dated 2nd August 2016 to Lucy Frazer.

5/11/2017   Mail — ██████████

Dishonesty and abuse of power of judges

paul osler

Tue 02/08/2016 14.54

To: lucy.frazer.mp@parliament.uk <lucy.frazer.mp@parliament.uk>;

Dear Mrs Frazer,

     I live in your constituency at ████████████████████ I am a retired solicitor and the founder of Oslers Solicitors which has offices in Stowmarket and Cambridge.

     I have recently conducted a civil case for a friend which started as a small claims track county court case which led on to an attempted appeal (permission to appeal refused) and then a Judicial Review (permission refused on "totally without merit" basis). It is a case which has troubled me greatly because it demonstrates a criminal dishonesty on the part of the three judges involved. The first judge, the District Judge, was biased and either deliberately ignored the law or was manifestly incompetent. The evidence points to the former. The appeal should have been a shoo-in since, in my opinion, it was bound to succeed on a number of points. The Circuit Judge refused permission to appeal stating none of the appeal points had any real prospect of success. That decision was demonstrably dishonest and, on the balance of probabilities, there is every reason to believe she discussed the appeal with the trial judge. I wrote a letter before action to the Circuit Judge (with a view to a judicial review) in which I accused her of having acted with bias toward the trial judge, of having colluded with her and of having breached her oath of office, ignored the law and acted to defeat justice. In that letter I called upon her to explain the reason for one part of her judgment which had led to my allegation that she had colluded with the trial judge but she declined to explain herself. There then followed a judicial review in which I repeated my accusations against the Circuit Judge and asked the Administrative Court to declare the appeal had been an unfair process and to quash the Circuit Judge's decision. It took six months for a decision on the papers to be given and when it came it was from a Deputy High Court judge who poured scorn on all my arguments and refused permission declaring the claim to be "totally without merit" thereby denying an oral hearing at which the application for permission could be renewed. I then made a complaint to the Judicial Conduct Investigations Office accusing the Deputy High Court judge of having been dishonest and of having acted to defeat justice and protect her fellow judges and the image of the judiciary. They declared my complaint invalid as it did not relate to "personal" misconduct (rudeness etc) and they could not investigate a judicial decision. I referred the matter to the Ombudsman complaining that the regulations did not limit misconduct to personal behaviour and indeed expressly allowed for complaint about a judicial decision. The Ombudsman has accepted that one can complain about a judicial decision where misconduct is alleged but, without dealing with my arguments on the point, has simply accepted the JCIO's interpretation of misconduct as being "personal" misconduct.

     Why then am I writing to you? Well, it was Parliament which gave us the Civil Procedure Rules and the right to fair appeals and when judges deliberately ignore that law they thwart the will of Parliament and take away our rights. If that is going on then one would expect Parliament to be somewhat peeved. Judges in practice are astonishingly unaccountable. They supervise themselves through appeals. They are immune from prosecution and civil suit relating to conduct in the course of their duties. The Judicial Conduct Investigations Office will only consider misconduct which is "personal" so they won't look at an allegation that a judge deliberately acted to defeat justice! I fear you too will be disinclined to get involved due to the separation of powers. Yet the Lord Chancellor and Parliament have power to look at misconduct by judges and the complaint is not about a judicial decision relating to a decision of the government. Presumably you could look at my complaint and draw it to the attention of others if you wished (perhaps one of the senior judges who like to tell us how great and good our judges are?).

     I can see that you might say that you have no time to look at individual cases; that you can't be seen to interfere with judicial decisions; that it is very unlikely that the three judges I refer to are all dishonest etc. Yet it is an individual case which can provide concrete evidence of a serious problem and surely you could draw this to the attention of the right people were you to agree with my analysis of the case. As to the likelihood of three judges being dishonest, you won't know unless you look at the evidence. Also, it is the very fact that such is unlikely that makes it so outrageous because it is not what we expect. Also relevant is the fact that I am legally qualified.

     Chris Huhne and Vicky Price went to prison for less yet these judges continue in their office untouched because they are untouchable when they act in concert. They are above the law.

     In summary, I am a retired solicitor informing you that I have a case which evidences that three judges have acted with bias, ignored the law and dishonestly defeated justice. In so doing they have defied the rule of law (see Bingham's 6th principle), the Magna Carta ("to no-one will we deny right or justice"), the criminal law (misconduct in a public office), the civil law (Negligence and general principles of causation and loss), statutory rules (The Civil Procedure Rules) and their oath of office. They cannot be prosecuted. They have ignored the will of Parliament and denied one of Her Majesty's subjects his rights knowingly causing him harm. The JCIO and the Ombudsman won't even recognise the validity of the complaint. I invite you to look at this case. I am happy to discuss it with you in person or in correspondence. Are you interested? If so, I will make the documents available to you (it is not voluminous).

https://outlook.live.com/owa/?id=64855&path=/mail/AQMkADAwATYwMAltOWI1Ni04NmMxLTAwAi0wMAoALgAAA7%2BRiI8f8hBKpn4OlEyWivMBAFd3... 1/2

"...there is no hope for the rule of law unless we have judges who are independent, honest, fair and competent.........It is self-evident that if judges are dishonest....the rule of law will be fatally undermined. If judges break the law, what possible hope is there that anyone else will bother to observe it?" Lord Neuberger at the Hong Kong Foreign Correspondents' Club 26th August 2014.

Paul Osler

b) Letter dated 3rd August 2016 from Lucy Frazer.

Lucy Frazer QC MP
HOUSE OF COMMONS
LONDON SW1A 0AA

Paul A Osler

3 August 2016

Dear Mr Osler,

Thank you for contacting me regarding issues you have faced during the appeals process. I am sorry to hear of your ongoing frustrations.

I am happy to assist you where I can. From your summary of the case it appears that you have already pursued the legitimate avenues to challenge judicial decisions and it is therefore difficult to see what further steps can be taken.

I will however write to the Minister for Courts and Justice, Sir Oliver Heald, to share your concerns and see if he has any further thoughts or ideas on the matters you raise.

Thank you again, and I will let you know when I receive a response.

Yours sincerely,

Lucy Frazer QC MP

c) Letter dated 13th September 2016 from Lucy Frazer, enclosing the letter from Dr Phillip Lee.

Lucy Frazer QC MP
HOUSE OF COMMONS
LONDON SW1A 0AA

Paul A Osler

13 September 2016

Dear Mr Osler,

As I mentioned in my letter to you of 3 August, I wrote to the Ministry of Justice regarding the concerns you raised over the appeals process. I have now received a response, a copy of which I have enclosed. I am sorry it is not more helpful.

Please do let me know if you think there might be anything else that I can do for you within my role as an MP.

Yours sincerely,

Lucy Frazer QC MP

d) Letter dated August 2016 from Dr Phillip Lee.

Ministry
of Justice

Dr Phillip Lee MP
Parliamentary Under-
Secretary of State for
Justice
Duty Minister

MoJ ref: ▮▮▮▮▮▮

Mrs Lucy Frazer MP
Member of Parliament for South East Cambridgeshire
House of Commons
London
SW1A 0AA

⋋   August 2016

Dear Lucy

ABUSE OF POWER BY JUDGES

Thank you for your letter of 3 August 2016 on behalf of your constituent, Mr Paul Osler ▮▮▮▮▮▮▮ ▮▮▮▮▮▮▮▮▮▮▮▮▮ regarding allegations of criminal dishonesty on the part of three judges. I am responding on behalf of my colleague, as I am the Duty Minister during this recess.

The Lord Chief Justice and the Lord Chancellor are jointly responsible for matters relating to judicial conduct and discipline. Their responsibilities cover matters relating to allegations of potential personal misconduct in the way a judicial office holder has behaved, whether inside or outside the courtroom. Their remit does not extend to considering matters relating to judicial decision and case management, including the application of the law. Complaints about judicial misconduct are handled in accordance with the provisions of the Judicial Discipline (Prescribed Procedures) Regulations 2014 and supporting rules. They are assisted in their duty by the Judicial Conduct Investigation Office (JCIO).

I note that Mr Osler's complaint was considered by the JCIO and a letter was sent to him on 28 June 2016 explaining that the matters he raised related to judicial decision and case management. This decision has also been upheld by the Judicial Appointments and Conduct Ombudsman. The Lord Chancellor and Lord Chief Justice have no powers to review the decisions Judges make or intervene in individual cases. Judges carry out their duties having regard only to the facts and arguments which are brought before them, and it is their task to apply the law in that light. Judicial decisions are for Judges and Judges alone. They are not answerable for their decisions in the same way a government minister is. A judge's decision may only be challenged by the parties to a case by way of an appeal or in some circumstances by judicial review.

I am sorry that I am unable to assist Mr Osler with his concerns in regards to his case.

DR PHILLIP LEE MP

e) My letter dated 21st September 2016 to Lucy Frazer.

Mr P A Osler,

21st September 2016

Lucy Frazer QC MP,
House of Commons,
London, SW1A 0AA.

Dear Mrs Frazer,

Re : Dishonest Judges

Thank you for your letter dated the 13th September.

The response from Dr Lee is very interesting because it shows the extent to which a basic misapplication of the law by the JCIO has become accepted. It is a misapplication that Mrs Judith Ankorn, a former head of the JCIO, is responsible for.

The JCIO has power to issue advice on the application and interpretation of the statutory rules relevant to complaints against judges. During her reign, Mrs Ankorn issued "Supplementary Guidance" which can still be found on the JCIO's website. That guidance states that one cannot complain about a judicial decision and it defines "misconduct" as "personal misconduct" (by which it means bad manners!). This view is now stated as an unarguable fact on the internet yet it is wholly misconceived. Rather than repeat my arguments fully here, I enclose a copy of the correspondence I have had with the JCIO and the Ombudsman.

When I complained to the Ombudsman, he would have seen from my complaint made against the High Court judge that I am a retired solicitor whereas those of the JCIO are not legally qualified. That does not, of course, mean I am right but one would have thought it invited a degree of respect and caution on his part. Not so. Having carried out only a preliminary investigation he found that "there is no prospect of any finding of maladministration" and my complaint did "not warrant a full investigation". Yet my complaint to the Ombudsman followed normal rules of statutory interpretation and common sense. The JCIO's arguments, on the other hand, did neither and, further, showed a failure to understand basic English and ran contrary to the statutory rules.

The rules state that one cannot complain about a judicial decision unless a question of misconduct is raised. As I say, basic English. In his rejection of my complaint, the Ombudsman accepted one can, where misconduct is raised, complain about a judicial decision but, without dealing with my arguments on the point, he just accepted that "misconduct" means "personal misconduct"! The reasoning used by the JCIO to conclude that one cannot complain about a judicial decision was the same used to support the notion that "misconduct" means "personal misconduct". Given the Ombudsman had clearly found that reasoning to be flawed re the first proposition, one would have thought he would treat it with a high degree of suspicion when looking at the second. Not so. He accepted the Supplementary Guidance issued by the JCIO as if it were the law in place of the statutory rules.

Subsequent to the Ombudsman's decision, I wrote again to the JCIO asking for the legal authority behind their definition of "misconduct". They replied confirming that they are simply relying on their power to advise on the application and interpretation of the rules i.e their Supplementary Guidance. They also said that their assertion that "misconduct" means "personal misconduct" flows directly from their view that one cannot complain about any

212

judicial decision. They reason that if one cannot complain about any judicial decision then it follows that "misconduct" can only mean "personal misconduct". In so doing, they are ignoring the Ombudsman's view that one can complain about a judicial decision.

Given that the Ombudsman found that one can complain about a judicial decision, I have written to him again asking him to revisit his determination of my complaint in light of the plainly flawed reasoning of the JCIO re "misconduct". I am not hopeful because the Ombudsman's initial decision evidences a clear bias on his part. If he is honest and impartial then surely he must revisit and change his decision given the JCIO's clarification as to their reasoning which is founded on a notion that the Ombudsman found to be wrong. We will see.

With this letter I have not included my letter of complaint against the High Court judge since the nature of that complaint is clear from the correspondence with the JCIO and the Ombudsman.

I could judicially review the JCIO or the Ombudsman but any remedy is discretionary and, even though the normal rule is that a decision which is the product of a misapplication of the law will be returned to the decision-maker, I have no confidence whatsoever that the court will act fairly. Indeed, I believe that it will find any excuse to deny me a remedy and then order me to pay tens of thousands of pounds in costs. I did invite the JCIO to allow a lawyer-free judicial review so there would be no costs risk on either side but they have advised they will fully contest the matter using Treasury Solicitors etc. It strikes me as odd that the JCIO would want to take up such a partisan and adversarial stance in this matter. Surely it is in the public interest that the court should give us a precedent on the correct interpretation?

Even if my complaint now moves forward, it will be dealt with by judges, which brings me back to the fact that judges collectively are above the law. I do not accept that MPs, Ministers and Parliament are unable to confront judges when they are plainly abusing their powers and depriving us of rights given to us by Parliament. A complaint to the JCIO is but one path to the disciplining of a judge. The "rights of the individual" are oft lauded yet they only exist when they do not conflict with the ultimate power holders. Per se, the individual is powerless. In China they neither have the form nor the substance of justice. Here we are cleverer because we have the form but, when it suits and those with power can get away with it, we lack the substance.

Yours sincerely,

Paul Osler

f) My email dated 27th September 2016 to Lucy Frazer.

10/11/2016   Dishonest judges - paul osler

Dishonest judges

paul osler

Tue 27/09/2016 17:58

To: lucy.frazer.mp@parliament.uk <lucy.frazer.mp@parliament.uk>;

Dear Mrs Frazer,

   in my letter to you of the 21st September, I advised that I had asked the Ombudsman to revisit his decision and I opined that if he were impartial and honest then he would surely do so. I attach his response dated the 26th September. Having previously ruled that one can complain about a judicial decision he appears now to be saying one cannot. In any event, the content of his letter is nonsense. Either he does not understand his role or he is biased and dishonest.

   In your letter to me you asked if there was anything else you could do for me in your role as MP. I may be reading too much into it but it occurred to me that you might think I had some other role in mind. I do not.

Regards,

Paul Osler

g) Letter dated 17th October 2016 from Lucy Frazer.

Lucy Frazer QC MP
HOUSE OF COMMONS
LONDON SW1A 0AA

Paul A Osler

17 October 2016

Dear Mr Osler,

Thank you for your letter of 21 September and your further email of 27 September. I am sorry that your case has not been satisfactorily resolved.

As the Ombudsman has already considered your case I am not sure how best I can assist. This is primarily a legal matter as I am sure you are aware. If you think that there is something I can do as your MP please do let me know as I would be happy to assist.

Thank you again for updating me.

Yours sincerely,

Lucy Frazer QC MP

APPENDIX G: Extract from *The Accountability of the Judiciary* dated October 2007, and my unanswered letter to the Judicial Office dated 9th April 2017 (contains public sector information licensed under the Open Government Licence v3.0.).

the responsibility of the judiciary set out in "d" is not inconsistent with the requirements of judicial independence.

"**e**":   One of the justifications for two levels of appeal (to the Court of Appeal and then to the House of Lords) is the particular responsibility of the judiciary in a common law system for developing the law.

To whom are individual judges and the judiciary accountable?

Four forms of accountability are considered:

- Internal accountability to more senior judges or courts by way of (a) the system of appeals against judicial decisions, and (b) procedures for dealing with complaints about the conduct of judges,

- External accountability to the public by way of amenability to scrutiny in particular by the media, but more widely by civil society,

- Accountability to the executive branch of the state (the Government), and

- Accountability to the legislative branch of the state (Parliament).

These forms of accountability overlap. For instance, the appeal and complaints processes provide both internal accountability and accountability to the public, and the giving of evidence to legislative committees provides direct accountability to Parliament and indirect accountability to the public.

The accountability of individual judges

Accountability to the executive of the state

Under the Act of Settlement 1701 and subsequent legislation (currently the Supreme Court Act 1981, section 11(3) as amended by the CRA) judges of the High Court and the Court of Appeal hold office during "good behaviour". This protection was given to protect judges against the power of the executive. These judges are not individually accountable to the executive in their capacity as such in either the "sacrificial" or the "explanatory" senses. It is axiomatic that safeguards on their tenure are a vital part of the independence of the judiciary.

That is not to say that the executive in the form of the Lord Chancellor has no role to play in the consideration of complaints and disciplinary proceedings made against judges. Such accountability, however, is subject to the limits set out in the CRA and the Concordat. The fundamentally important requirement is that the Lord Chancellor and the Lord Chief Justice have to agree before a judge is removed or disciplined in some other way. The fact that both have a role ensures that the independence of an individual judge is not improperly infringed, either by the executive, or internally by another member of the judiciary.

Accountability to the legislative branch of the state

As has been stated, both Houses of Parliament have the power, originating in the Act of Settlement, to petition the Queen for the removal of a judge of the High Court and the Court of Appeal, i.e. the ultimate form of accountability. It has not been exercised in modern history.

Turning to other forms of accountability, subject to a rule ("the *sub judice* rule") preventing the discussion of ongoing cases, the decisions and conduct of individual judges may be mentioned in debates in either House. This, however, does not mean that judges are accountable to Parliament for their decisions in particular cases, save insofar as Parliament may legislate to reverse the effect of a decision (on which see below). Accountability for their decisions is incompatible with judges' necessary independence.

Individual judges may also be invited to give evidence to Parliamentary Committees. Under Standing Orders, Select Committees and their sub-Committees have power to "send for persons, papers and records" relevant to their terms of reference. In modern times judges who have been asked to attend have done so voluntarily, subject to the well-established and long-standing rules and conventions that prevent judges from commenting on certain matters. [7] Parliamentary Committees respect these rules and conventions. The prohibited matters include; the merits of government policy, the merits of individual cases whether involving that judge or other judges, or of particular serving judicial officers, politicians and other public figures, and the merits, meaning or likely effect of provisions in prospective legislation.

Internal accountability to "the judiciary"

In the sense that their decisions are subject to appeal and other judges are responsible for the allocation of cases to them, individual judges are accountable to senior judges or judges holding positions of responsibility. As for the conduct of judges, a working group established by the Judges' Council published a *Guide to Judicial Conduct* in October 2004.[8] This seeks to provide guidance on matters such as; impartiality, integrity, competence and diligence, personal relationships and perceived bias and activities outside the court.

The responsibilities of the Heads of Division, Presiding, Resident and Family Liaison and Chancery Supervision Judges, and judges in charge of a particular jurisdiction, are designed to assist in the effective management of judicial work.[9] They must be exercised with due regard to the importance of the need to respect the independence of individual judges in relation to the decisions before them. This means, for example, that they cannot tell another judge how to decide a case. Decisions as to listing and allocation are designed to ensure that cases are heard by an appropriate judge and that the available judiciary is fully and effectively deployed within the resources provided by the executive branch of the state. It is to be observed, however, that one of the guarantees of independence under Article 6 of the European Convention of Human Rights, reflecting underlying common law principle, is that judges must be free from outside instructions or pressure from other members of the court or the judiciary. This limits the extent and form of discipline to which a judge may be subjected.

Accountability to the public

The formal processes of court proceedings provide a form of accountability to the public enabling scrutiny of the work of individual judges. As a general rule court proceedings and the decisions of judges are made in public. Decisions must be reasoned, and are subject to comment, often robust comment, by the media and other commentators. The quality of individual decisions is also subject to control in the form of appeal to higher courts against alleged errors. This identification and correction of error by appellate courts is also public and reasoned.

Complaints against the personal conduct of the judiciary (other than against decisions in proceedings) are handled by the Office for Judicial Complaints. Ultimately a report is made to the Lord Chief Justice and Lord Chancellor. Complaints about the handling of such complaints can be made to the Judicial Appointments and Conduct Ombudsman.

---

[7] *Guidance to judges agreed by the Judicial Executive Board in July 2006 is available on the judiciary's website (www.judiciary.gov.uk).*

[8] *Available on the judiciary's website.*

[9] See *The Responsibilities of Resident Judges and Designated Civil and Family Judges* (July 2004), esp. paragraphs 9, 10(a) and 11(a). *Available on the judiciary's website.*

9th April 2017

Judicial Office,
11th Floor, Thomas More Building,
Royal Courts of Justice,
Strand,
London WC2A 2ll.

Dear Sirs,

Re: Judicial Accountability

I am writing a book which, in part, deals with judicial accountability.

On the Courts and Tribunals Judiciary website I have come across a document entitled "The Accountability of the Judiciary" which bears the logo and heading of the Judiciary of England and Wales and the date "October 2007". On page 7, under the heading "Accountability to the public", it is said: "Complaints against the personal conduct of the judiciary (other than against decisions in proceedings) are handled by the Office for Judicial Complaints. This notion of "personal conduct" is repeated again on page 10. This document post-dates The Constitutional Reform Act 2005 but not The Judicial Discipline (Prescribed Procedures) Regulations 2014 or The Judicial Conduct (Judicial and other office holders) Rules 2014 which are subordinate legislation made under that statute. The words "other than against decisions in proceedings" is contrary to Rule 21(b) of the statutory rules (see below).

On the Judicial Conduct and Investigations Office website, the idea that one can only complain about the personal conduct of judges is repeated. The JCIO has tried to explain this by referring to Rule 21(b) of the above-mentioned statutory rules which says that a complaint against a judge must be dismissed if "it is about a judicial decision or judicial case management, and raises no question of misconduct". The JCIO interpret this to mean one can never complain about a judicial decision and therefore misconduct can only mean personal misconduct. That is clearly not what the rule says. The rule is clear that one can complain about a judicial decision but an allegation of misconduct must be included. Given that personal misconduct would not affect the quality or validity of a judicial decision (one would never complain *about* a judicial decision because of personal misconduct – one would simply complain about the misconduct) it seems clear that, when complaining about a judicial decision, the rule envisages misconduct which is not personal (e.g. if it were clear that a judge had ignored the law and acted to defeat justice). That view is supported by the fact that neither the statute, the regulations nor the rules define misconduct as personal misconduct. It seems clear that whereas judges are immune from civil suit and prosecution they are not immune from complaint where their decision involves misconduct which is not personal.

Can you direct me to a legal authority in support of the proposition that misconduct means only personal misconduct (rudeness, misuse of status etc)? As far as I can tell, this definition has been created ultra vires by the JCIO and in contravention of the legislation.

Who wrote the document on your website to which I have referred and what is its authority?

In anticipation, thank you for your assistance with this matter.

Yours faithfully,

Paul Osler